PRAISE FOR *THE POWER OF PLAY*

"In an era of consumerism and parental pressure, Dr. Elkind defends that most wonderful aspect of childhood—our children's chance to dream and to make this a wonderful world for them and for us."—T. Berry Brazelton, M.D.

"Elkind argues that . . . when we take away time from playful learning, we deprive kids of important opportunities for emotional, intellectual, and moral growth."—*Teacher Magazine*

"Every parent should read this book . . . [Elkind] makes a coherent, readable, and altogether fascinating case."—John Rosemond

"Dr. Elkind suggests fun ways to get kids thinking (that don't involve homework and books)."—*Woman's Day*

"[A] fascinating look at the importance of letting kids be kids . . . With clarity and insight, Elkind calls for society to bring back long recesses, encourage imagination, and let children develop their minds at a natural pace."—*Publishers Weekly* (starred review)

"Drawing on diverse sources . . . [*The Power of Play*] is full of helpful discussions and examples."—*Choice*

"*The Power of Play* should be considered one of the primers for good parenting."—*Chicago Parent*

"Should be required reading for every parent . . . Elkind's thorough research and carefully reasoned presentation serve to emphasize the importance and good sense of what he has to say."—*Provo Daily Herald*

"One last shot at convincing American society about the dangers of the disappearing childhood." — *Tampa Tribune*

"Elkind, one of today's psychologists, shows that it is through play that learning happens. He provides guidance for wise use of kids' screen time, developmental understanding, and most interestingly, the use of good humor in parenting." — *Nashville Parent*

"A timely book on the importance of unstructured play in the academic preparation and development of children . . . Highly recommended." — *Library Journal* (starred review)

"Reassuring . . . Dr. Elkind talks about how to reintroduce creative, imaginative play into your child's life." — *Scholastic Parent and Child*

"Elkind offers simple, practical guidance for parents and educators who would combine love, work, and play to foster health, intelligence, and creativity in children." — *American School Board Journal*

PRAISE FOR *THE HURRIED CHILD*

"A landmark book." — *Chicago Sun-Times*

"David Elkind [is] one of psychology's leading lights." — *Washington Post*

"[O]ffers excellent perspectives on children, parents, and culture . . . this powerful book is essential reading." — *Library Journal*

"[Elkind's] main theme remains relevant more than 25 years after its initial publishing." — *The Jewish Week*

PARENTING
on the go

Also by David Elkind

The Power of Play

The Hurried Child

Reinventing Childhood

All Grown Up and No Place to Go

Ties That Stress

Parenting Your Teenager

A Sympathetic Understanding of the Child

Understanding Your Child: Birth to Sixteen

Images of the Young Child

Grandparenting: Understanding Today's Children

Miseducation

Children and Adolescents

The Child's Reality: Three Developmental Themes

The Child and Society

Child Development and Education

Giants in the Nursery (in press)

ELK

PARENTING
on the go

Birth to Six,
A to Z

David Elkind

Da Capo
LIFE
LONG

A Member of the Perseus Books Group

Designed by Trish Wilkinson
Set in 11.5 point Minion Pro by the Perseus Books Group

Library of Congress Cataloging-in-Publication Data

Elkind, David, 1931–
   Parenting on the go : birth to six, A to Z / David Elkind.
      pages cm
   ISBN 978-0-7382-1750-5 (paperback) — ISBN 978-0-7382-1751-2 (e-book)
1. Child rearing—Handbooks, manuals, etc. 2. Parenting—Handbooks, manuals, etc. 3. Infants—Development. 4. Child development. I. Title.
HQ769.E5534 2014
305.231—dc23   2014008660

First Da Capo Press edition 2014

Published by Da Capo Press
A Member of the Perseus Books Group
www.dacapopress.com

Note: The information in this book is true and complete to the best of our knowledge. This book is intended only as an informative guide for those wishing to know more about health issues. In no way is this book intended to replace, countermand, or conflict with the advice given to you by your own physician. The ultimate decision concerning care should be made between you and your doctor. We strongly recommend you follow his or her advice. Information in this book is general and is offered with no guarantees on the part of the authors or Da Capo Press. The authors and publisher disclaim all liability in connection with the use of this book. The names and identifying details of people associated with events described in this book have been changed. Any similarity to actual persons is coincidental.

Da Capo Press books are available at special discounts for bulk purchases in the U.S. by corporations, institutions, and other organizations. For more information, please contact the Special Markets Department at the Perseus Books Group, 2300 Chestnut Street, Suite 200, Philadelphia, PA, 19103, or call (800) 810-4145, ext. 5000, or e-mail special.markets@perseusbooks.com.

10 9 8 7 6 5 4 3 2 1

To my three sons, Paul, Rob, and Rick,
who gave me my first lessons in Parenting on the Go.

Contents

Contents

T. 231

Contents

Introduction

I believe that in contemporary American society we have a time famine. This is particularly true for single- or two-parent working families with young children. Finding hours to shop, housekeep, and do home maintenance, prepare meals, do laundry (never mind have a personal life)—and still have time for eating, reading, and playing with one's children becomes a monster task of scheduling.

The time famine is aided and abetted by a generation gap produced by the phenomenal rate of technological change. Even a century ago, parents could pretty much rear their children as they had been reared. That is no longer true. Many contemporary parents did not themselves grow up with the internet, texting, touch-screen technology and tablets.

To address these issues, several years ago Mark Hamilton and Michele Hamilton created *Just Ask Baby*, a series of short online videos in which an infant, Joey, talks to his parents about the social, emotional, and intellectual development problems he is experiencing in the first year of life. He suggests to the two actor parents, who are also in the video, how best to handle them.

I wrote the scripts for the series, and also two 500-word weekly blogs which subscribers to *Just Ask Baby* got as a bonus. I did this for two years. The blogs covered a wide range of issues pertinent to the rearing of young children. For a variety of reasons, *Just Ask Baby* did not catch on and was discontinued.

It seemed to me, however, that another way to approach the time famine for the parents of young children was to put the blogs together as a handy reference guide that they could turn to for quick answers to immediately pressing problems.

Today's parents don't often have time to consult parenting books, but they could use a short, to-the-point discussion of the challenges they meet daily.

It was with this goal in mind that I put together *Parenting on the Go: Ages Birth to Six, A to Z*. I feel comfortable in offering this guide because I have worked as a child clinical psychologist in departments of psychiatry, in the public schools, as head of a child study center; as a consultant to child guidance clinics; and as a psychologist in juvenile courts. I have also had a small private practice. At the same time, I have conducted research and taught as a professor of child development at several major universities (thirty years at Tufts) and as an author/lecturer, speaking to parents and teachers in the United States and abroad.

Together these experiences have taught me that parents are in much more need of guidance than they were in the past. Yet they have less time and less practical experience, because they come from smaller families than earlier generations did. That is why I believe a brief, authoritative guide to the multitude of early childhood issues is appropriate for information-age parents.

Because the book will be an e-book as well as a print book, parents can refer to it on their handheld devices. This makes the guide accessible when they are away from home.

A word about organization. I have tried to label the topics in the way I think most parents would look for them. For example, I titled a piece "Special Needs Children," rather than "Children with Special Needs," and "Autism Spectrum Disorders," rather than "Children with Autism." But I may not always have judged it right, so if you don't find what you are looking for, try some other related words.

A

Acid Reflux

At a book signing recently, a mother asked me to sign a book for her friend who couldn't come herself. The mother explained that her friend's baby had acid reflux and had to be constantly attended to. Inasmuch as it is a common affliction, it seemed reasonable to write about.

GERD, or gastro-esophageal reflex disorder, occurs in about 50 percent of infants (it occurs in children and adults as well) but varies in severity. Basically what happens is that stomach contents move back up the tube—the esophagus—that connects the stomach with the mouth. This happens when a ring at the bottom of the esophagus, which allows food and drink to enter the stomach, closes prematurely.

In many infants this happens because this ring is not fully developed. The food may back up when the infant is burped. But sometimes it happens by itself and is evidenced by spitting, repeated vomiting, coughing, and poor feeding. Sometimes the reflex results in projectile vomiting. In the vast majority of children the problem disappears when the muscles are more fully developed.

If you suspect that your infant has GERD, it is best to check with your pediatrician and learn from him or her what might be the cause, and which course of treatment to follow. He or she may recommend a number of possible causes and remedies for an infant who is suffering from severe GERD. It has been found, for example, that babies with acid reflux have fewer and less severe symptoms when they are breast-fed than when they are fed only formula. Human milk is digested more easily and is emptied from the stomach twice as quickly. When the stomach is emptied quickly, acid reflux is less likely. Human milk may also be less irritating to the esophagus.

If breast-feeding is not possible for one reason or another, your pediatrician may suggest alternatives. If the child has a protein milk allergy, eliminating cow's milk from the diet will often solve the problem in a mere twenty-four hours. Switching to Enfamil or Similac may also solve the problem for these infants. For infants with protein intolerance, a switch to a formula using NeoCate or Elecare may help reduce or eliminate the symptoms.

Some pediatricians suggest thickening the formula with a tablespoon of rice, which can also decrease vomiting. If you do this, enlarge the hole in the nipple of the baby's bottle to make it work. Another strategy is to hold your infant's head on your shoulder for 20 to 30 minutes after feeding. This helps to ensure that the food goes down and that the ring does not close prematurely.

For infants with uncomplicated GERD, most symptoms are resolved by the end of the first year and usually earlier.

Allergies

A while ago I gave a talk at the Children's Museum in Greenville, NC—an exceptionally fine example of what this kind of museum should be. During the talk my throat suddenly felt like I had swallowed a fluff ball. The audience was immediately sympathetic. Although Greenville is a truly beautiful city, it is also the pollen capital of the United States. It reminded in a very dramatic way that spring is a high allergy season.

About one in four children in the US suffer from one form of allergy or another. My oldest son had asthma from birth, so I am well familiar with stresses an allergic child can place on parents. What we went through provides something of a guide for what all parents who have children with allergies will have to cope with. For example, when we found that Paul was allergic to animals, I had to give away my dog, a dog I got as a pup and had had for years even before my wife and I were married. It also meant that we could not take Paul to the homes of friends who had animals, and that he could not visit his own friends if they had pets.

But that is just the beginning. Because Paul was, and still is, allergic to nuts, we had to be very careful about the foods he ate. We found that we had to read the ingredients of a lot of snack foods which did not advertise having nuts but did have them in one form or another. He could also not be around people who smoked. At that time, this included many people, including his parents. So we gave up smoking—sometimes good things come out of bad—and had a central air filter put on our heating system.

Pollen season was often the most difficult for him, leading to sinus infections, crankiness, and general low mood. But the worst was when he accidently ate something that brought on an asthma attack and we had to rush him to the hospital.

With time we developed strategies to cope with the situation and to make life as livable as possible for us all, including his two younger brothers, who did not have asthma. We had to be careful not to pay so much attention to Paul that his brothers would feel that he was favored.

The most important thing, we discovered, was to get a competent, experienced doctor to give us a correct reading of the problem. We moved to Rochester, NY, when Paul was four and found a specialist, who gave him a series of tests and then prescribed regular shots that worked like vaccines to keep the asthma in check. After taking the shots, Paul had many fewer attacks and less severe symptoms. So getting the best medical help available is the most important first step in dealing with an asthmatic child or one who has allergies.

We learned a few other things as well:

1. For a while we limited our social life for fear that Paul might have an attack while we were away. Once he was on the shots, we found a competent babysitter who had our phone number and the doctor's in case there was an emergency. If we had continued to limit our social life, we might have begun to resent Paul for it.

2. We sometimes used the allergy as an excuse not to go to a function or social gathering we really did not want to attend. But that ploy is easily seen through, and we got a lot of pushback when did that, so we stopped using that tactic except in the extreme case. And we didn't let Paul get away with it either.

3. We learned to be flexible—to adjust our plans if we foresaw a potentially risky situation.

4. We made sure that asthma did not become the central point of family life. Asthma and allergies are a reality, and we have to deal with them. But they should not dictate family routines and schedules. Too much coddling of an allergic or an asthmatic child is not healthy for the child nor for the rest of the family.

Apps for Toddlers

It was bound to happen: the touch screen and the tablet have done for preschoolers' intellectual environment what Montessori's child-sized chairs and cutlery did for their physical environment. They removed the barriers to learning things that were within the range of their mental abilities but outside the range of their physical ones. The touch screen and tablets did this by allowing young children to maneuver a large object on the screen with their fingertips that would be impossible, or very difficult, for them to move in the real world.

There is now a wide variety of apps for preschoolers. The Tosca Boca Company has put out a number of appealing programs like Tea Party, which allows the child to set the table and pour the tea, etc.

A much more direct academic approach has been taken by 24x7digital, which put out TeachMe: Kindergarten, among others. These apps aim at teaching young children pre-reading, pre-math, and pre-spelling skills. Again, the touch screen makes it possible for young children to manipulate images of things they could not manage as real objects. In addition, most of the programs are self-correcting, so if the child makes the wrong choice, he or she is encouraged to go back and try again.

The question is, Just because we can do something—for example, create apps for toddlers—should we do it? From a strictly commercial point of view, the answer is clearly yes. These apps can be marketed as educational and thus play on parental guilt and anxiety about their children's readiness to live in a digital world. The question of whether using these apps is educational or beneficial is not so easily answered.

One of the difficulties, as journalist Hanna Rosin points out, is that we tend to approach these questions from the adult point of view. We look at such apps as either educational or simply fun, and fail to appreciate that for young children there is no difference between having fun and learning; for them, learning is fun, and if they are having fun, they are learning. For young children, everything is new and exciting; living is learning.

From this perspective, touch screen apps are really not much different from the play gyms that hang above cribs and allow the child to interact with them. When an infant hits a rattle hanging from the gym, it makes a sound. And when they move something on a screen by touching it, there is not much difference from the child's point of view. You touch or act upon something, and something happens.

For the young child, therefore, the touch screen is no different from any other interactive toy, such as a rattle. And like other toys, young children will use them for a while and eventually move on to something more novel and interesting. Put differently, the touch screen is truly different for us adults, who never experienced them as children. But for the child who has no historical perspective, the touch screen is just another part of his or her interactive world.

So we really shouldn't worry about whether the touch screen apps are educational or not. If the child enjoys playing with apps, then the only concern we should have is that the child not become addicted to them. This is unlikely, since the novelty of apps, like the novelty of many other toys, soon wears off.

The only toys with lasting value are such things as wooden or plastic blocks, which allow children to actually use their hands to create new structures. While learning with icons can be interesting and fun, nothing beats the sense of dealing with real things.

Argue, Children Who

In their book *Getting to Yes*, Roger Fisher, William Ury, and Bruce Patten describe a number of negotiating strategies that can be used in many different situations. Although the book was written for adult negotiators, I believe many of the principles outlined in that book can work just as well for negotiations between parents and children. One of the most important of these is the idea that you must focus upon some general rule or principle in negotiating, and avoid arguments based on emotion.

For example, some children are what might be called "persisters"; they keep repeating the same request, and sometimes they may catch you off guard. A child may, for example, want something that other children have—a type of clothing or electronic gadget—which may be too expensive for the family budget, or something that you believe to be unnecessary or inappropriate for children of that age.

The child's usual argument is: "Everybody else has one." One type of reply is: "So if everyone else catches cold does that mean you want to catch cold too?" A rule based reply, however, might be: "In this family we don't buy things just because other people do." Whenever the child makes a similar request, we need only remind him or her of the rule.

With younger children, you can use a similar strategy. While shopping at the grocery store, the child may ask for a lot things, including candy. One rule might be: "When we go shopping, you get to pick one thing, but it can't cost more than a dollar." If the child wants more than one thing, you need to remind him or her of the rule.

The same general strategy can be used to deal with arguments between siblings. In this situation, it is important to begin by saying, "In this family both sides to an argument get to have their say. I want to hear both sides, without yelling, screaming, or name-calling. You have to let the other person talk without interruption, and you will be offered the same courtesy."

Once both sides have had their say, you are ready to look for a general rule or principle. If the argument is, say, over which TV program to watch, the principle might be that each child gets to watch a program of his or her choice. The task then is to work out a schedule so each child gets to watch a favorite show. The important thing is to move the discussion from the personal (who is right or wrong, bad or good) to some objective, practical solution.

Parenting involves a lot of negotiation. Learning to negotiate on the basis of rules rather than emotions is a very good strategy for parents to employ and for children to learn.

Assemble Kids' Toys?

I am sure I share the experience of many grandparents and parents who have encountered packaging for toys for their grandchildren or children with the ominous label "some assembly required." The label becomes infuriating after it is removed from under the tree and the holiday wrappings are removed.

For example, someone purchased a pink roadster for my granddaughter Heather's Disney Princess doll to ride in. The first problem was getting it out of the hard plastic packaging, which I eventually had to cut open with a shears. Then a lot of the pieces were tied to cardboard backing, and these too had to be cut out. And this was before I started putting the thing together. There were a lot of little pieces, and I had to be careful to keep them out of the reach of Heather's baby sister.

The number of toys with the label "some assembly required" has increased over the years, mainly for economic reasons. Unassembled toys are cheaper to ship than are assembled toys. They also take up less space on the shelves of toy stores, so a greater variety of kids' playthings can be displayed.

For most young children, like my granddaughter, putting together a toy is not what they are interested in. They want toys that they can play with right from the box. That is why Papa (me) gets asked to put the assembly-required toys together. Toys that kids can see but not play with frustrate young children. In my opinion, such toys are more trouble than they are worth.

The assembly-required toys have to be distinguished from a very different type of plaything, namely, the construction toy, such as Legos. Construction toys are made for children to put together and at one time had no pre-determined end result. For example, Lego only suggested things children could make with the blocks in the past, but now children are given instructions for making fairly complex machines.

In so doing, Lego has transformed the blocks from a creative, individual toy to one which requires the child to recreate what someone else has already designed and put together. While reproducing what someone else made has value, it does take away the child's initiative to build something of his or her own devising.

Construction toys have become big sellers in recent years, perhaps because of an effort to counter children's preoccupation with television and computer toys.

It should also be said that there are some toys, which should be assembled in advance by parents or grandparents. I am thinking here of a tricycle, small bicycle, or scooter, which might require adult tools for the assembly. It is best to present these vehicles to children as finished products.

Certainly there are some children who like to read and to follow instructions. For these children, some assembly-required toys can be stimulating and fun. But for most young children such toys are simply a tease. Given the preponderance of such toys, parents may have little choice. But if you do purchase such toys, it might be best to assemble them before wrapping them. It will make your child or grandchild's holiday experience a much happier and merrier one.

Athletes, Young

Entering young children into organized team sports has become the norm in the United States. It is estimated that almost 80 percent of children in the US participate in some form of organized sports. And this is happening at younger and younger ages. So-called T-ball is a case in point. Little League organizers were concerned that they were losing prospective players to soccer, a game that could be played by younger children. To get children into baseball earlier they introduced T-ball in which the ball is not pitched to the batter but is rather placed on a stationary post. Even young children can hit a ball when it is not moving. Some T-ball teams involve children as young as four, and some soccer teams do as well.

When I ask parents of young children why they put them on teams at an early age, the most frequent answer is, "All the other children in the neighborhood are on the team, and if my son/daughter is not on the team, he or she won't have any friends to play with."

As long as the children are having fun and not being asked to do anything that might put their bodies at risk, participation in sports at an early age need not be problem. In reality, it is just an organized group play date. It is only when parents and coaches get too enthusiastic and become more concerned about winning the game than about the children playing it, that sports for children become a problem.

It is simply a fact that young children's bones are not fully calcified and their muscles have not attained full volume. Vigorous sports can severely stress undeveloped bones and muscles. Each summer the emergency room at Boston Children's Hospital admits hundreds of children as a result of sports injuries.

In addition to the physical risks, there are psychological risks as well. A child who has been playing soccer or baseball since the age of four or five may burn out by the time he or she is an adolescent—when he or she might well excel at the sport.

Some parents tell me that they need to put their children in sports early so they can excel when they get older. But there is no more truth in this than in the idea that early academics will give young children an edge when they get older. It is interesting that while we have more than three million young people in Little League, an increasing number of players in the Major Leagues are from the Caribbean, Latin American, or Asia. In those countries (at least until recently) young people played baseball on their own and for fun. That appears to be the real road to later excellence in sports.

Other parents bring up the example of Tiger Woods, who started playing golf when he was two. Yet Tiger Woods is the exception, not the rule. He had tremendous talent to begin with. Recall a story about Mozart, who was asked by an aspiring composer to teach him how to write a symphony. Mozart replied that a symphony was a very complex work, and the young composer would be well advised to start with something simpler, like an étude. The young composer, somewhat put off, replied, "But Mozart, you wrote a symphony when you were eight." Mozart replied, "Yes, but I didn't have to ask how."

If young children participate in sports for fun and socialization, there is no problem. But if they are playing as preparation for becoming athletes, the activity may do more harm than good.

Attachment, Understanding

In my talks with parents, one of the most frequent subjects I get asked about is the nature of attachment. The questions often give evidence of two common misunderstanding about attachment, namely that a child becomes more attached to a caregiver than to a parent, and that the parent is solely responsible for the quality of the parent-child bond. Resolving these two misunderstandings requires a brief review of the theory of attachment and research on it.

The concept of attachment was introduced by psychiatrist and psychoanalyst John Bowlby. It is based on evolutionary theory and ethnographic research. Bowlby argued that infants need, after the first six months of life, to establish a bond with a caregiver who interacts with them socially in a sensitive and caring way. This interaction enables the infant to attach to the caregiver, and provides the infant with the emotional and social security to actively explore his or her world. From an evolutionary point of view, attachment is necessary for survival. In the usual case, the mother tends to be the attachment figure, but this can be anyone who consistently provides sensitive social interactions with the infant.

Attachment is assessed by a procedure introduced by psychologist Mary Ainsworth called *the strange situation test.* An infant is placed in a room with his or her mother. How the infant behaves when a stranger enters the room and interacts with the mother, and when the mother leaves the room, provide indices of the type of attachment the infant has to the parent.

Securely attached children show some stress when the mother leaves, but they freely explore the environment in her absence and show happiness on her return. Avoidant-insecure infants show little distress when the mother leaves, are reluctant to explore, and show little preference for the mother over a complete stranger. Resistant-insecure (ambivalent) children show little independent exploration, great separation anxiety, and an ambivalent response to the mother on her return.

The important point is that the infant attaches to primarily one person, and that is usually the mother. For it is the mother, or father, who provides the most consistent 24/7 care—weekends, holidays, and when the child is ill. Parents provide more care, and more individual care, than can be provided by a day care provider. A baby becomes securely attached to parents who consistently talk, sing, and cuddle the baby, as well as seeing to his or her nutritional and toileting needs.

A number of studies have shown that the kind of attachment the infant has during infancy has long-lasting effects. Securely attached infants are likely to be more emotionally secure and socially competent as adults than are children with the other types of attachment. There is, however, another variable that has to be added to this equation: the baby's temperament. That is to say, attachment is not entirely determined by the kind of care given to the infant.

Research has shown that some infant temperamental differences are present from birth and cannot be attributed to caregiver behavior. One has to assume, for example, that an infant who is "slow to warm up" (not responsive to parental affection) or is "difficult" (constantly fussy and cranky) would attach less easily than would "easy to please babies" (who respond with smiles and coos to parental attention) regardless of caregiver behavior. Indeed, infant temperamental differences can affect parental behavior. A warm, giving mother for example, might well feel rejected by a difficult child and become more cautious in her relationship with her child.

In summary, attachment is a very important parent-child dynamic, but it has to be remembered that it is a two-way street and that the child has as much to do with the quality of the attachment as the primary caregiver does.

I believe that this is particularly important to remember because it is ignored by those who advocate so-called attachment parenting. There is no guarantee that any style of parenting will trump temperamental differences. Parents who use such parenting without success may blame themselves and not learn the strategies that are most successful with temperamentally difficult or slow-to-warm-up children.

Attention Deficit Hyperactivity Disorder (ADHD)

Health professionals use the initialism "ADHD" to refer to a spectrum of disorders found in both children and adults. The symptoms of ADHD themselves are not necessarily a sign of disorder. It is only when these symptoms are excessive and/or age-inappropriate that they are indicative of a problem. All children, to illustrate, may fail to pay attention at home or at school sometimes. But for children with ADHD, attentional problems are the rule rather than the exception. Likewise, all children tend to be active, but children with ADHD are constantly in motion. Because these behavioral traits are chronic, they contribute to difficulties in relationships and in learning, both at home and at school.

Because ADHD is a basket of symptoms, at least six attentional and six activity difficulties have to be identified before making the diagnosis. A child with an attention deficit disorder has to consistently show six or more of the following symptoms:

- Difficulty following instructions
- Difficulty keeping attention on work or play activities both at home and at school
- Difficulty keeping attention on work or play both at home and at school
- Loses things needed for activities at home and at school
- Appears not to listen

- Doesn't pay close attention to details
- Seems disorganized
- Has trouble with tasks that take planning ahead
- Forgets things
- Is easily distracted

To be diagnosed with hyperactivity, the child must consistently show at least six of the following behaviors:

- Fidgety behavior
- Running or climbing inappropriately
- Unable to play quietly
- Blurts out answers
- Interrupts people
- Can't remain seated
- Talks too much
- Is always on the go
- Has trouble waiting his or her turn

Although these behaviors may give you a guide to whether your child has ADHD, the diagnosis should be made by a health professional—either a pediatrician or a clinical psychologist. If the diagnosis is made, a treatment program needs to be set up. This should be a combination of psychological and medical interventions.

ADHD children benefit from having a lot of structure and clear expectations both at home and at school. Parent counseling is also valuable. A pediatrician may also prescribe some activity depressants, such as Ritalin. It is very important to be careful about dosage, particularly over weekends and holidays. Used in combination with parental counseling and school cooperation, medication has been helpful in improving children's school performance.

Research workers have found that children with ADHD do not have enough of the brain chemicals that are essential for organizing thought. As a result, the brain does not work as well as it should. It has been found that ADHD runs in families, which is consistent with the brain explanation. Substance abuse and smoking during pregnancy have also been associated with ADHD.

Although ADHD is never cured, individuals with this syndrome learn to adapt to their limitations and devise ways to cope. Some individuals with ADHD have been able to achieve significant success as adults.

Autism Spectrum Disorders (ASD)

Autism spectrum disorders now affect approximately three out every 1,000 three- to four-year-old children in the United States. ASD diagnosis covers a wide range of children, from those who are quite seriously impaired to those who have a milder form of the disorder (called Asperger's Syndrome) and are not seriously disabled.

Doctors can usually make a reliable diagnosis of children with ASD by three years of age, but in many cases it can be accurately identified by the end of the first year. Parents are usually the first to notice that there is something wrong with the way the baby is reacting. The baby may be unresponsive to people and focus on a single item for long periods of time.

In other cases, the first signs of ASD can appear unexpectedly in children who seem to be developing normally. Parents recognize that something is wrong when a happy, babbling baby suddenly resists social interaction and becomes silent. While the causes of ASD are not fully understood, it is an area of active research. There is some evidence that there is a genetic component to the disorder and that it is related to a brain dysfunction in the first months of life.

Children with ASD can usually be identified because they do not follow the usual patterns of development. Three major characteristics set these children apart from other youngsters of the same age. ASD children (1) fail to relate well to people, even their parents, (2) manifest defective communication skills, and (3) often engage in overly repetitive behaviors or interests.

Sometimes ASD children may respond violently to certain sounds, smells, or the way objects look. It is also true that some children may appear normal in their development until the second or third year, when they lose the social and language skills they had acquired earlier. Now the child avoids social interaction and eye contact and begins to engage in very repetitive behaviors.

Many ASD children manifest unique musical or mathematical talents. (Recall the movie *Rain Man*, with Dustin Hoffman as the numerically brilliant autistic adult.) Such children and other high-level functioning autistic children with less severe symptoms have been described as having Asperger's Syndrome.

There is general agreement among physicians that early intervention is the best way to treat children with ASD. Because a variety of intervention programs is available, parents have to explore their options to ensure that the program they choose is best suited to the needs of their child.

Many communities now provide intervention programs for both families and schools. Such programs focus on improving the child's social and communication skills. Children with

Asperger's Syndrome and other high-level functioning ASD children are now included in regular classrooms.

The long-term effects of ASD depend upon the severity of the condition and the effectiveness of the interventions the child has received.

B

Baby in the Car

No parent intentionally forgets leaving an unattended infant in a car or SUV. Too often, however, hurried, harassed, and distracted—yet otherwise responsible and caring parents—inadvertently forget a child in a parked vehicle. Infants and young children can die of hyperthermia within a few hours even on a day that is not especially hot. The National Safety Council reports that some thirty infants and children die each year as a result of being left alone in a vehicle for long periods.

Although this issue has been consistently addressed in local media, it did not garner national attention until the publication of Gene Weingartner's article in the *Washington Post* called "Fatal Distraction." In that article Weingartner raised the question of whether leaving an infant or a young child alone in a vehicle was a crime. She won the 2010 Pulitzer Prize for Feature Writing for her article.

"Fatal Distraction" has increased parental awareness of the risks of leaving infants unattended in vehicles. As more and more children are placed in the back seats to protect them from front-seat airbag injury, the likelihood of their being forgotten has increased. So too has pressure on the auto industry to find devices for reminding drivers that a child has been left behind.

An advocacy group, Kids and Cars, has tried, so far unsuccessfully, to get legislation to force manufacturers to include such devices. The auto industry has not made a great voluntary effort to deal with the issue, and it has not yet come up with a fail-safe technical solution. One reason that the auto industry has not put too much effort into finding a warning device is the liability threat. If the device fails to work, the company in question would be liable for the resulting death.

Although Kids and Cars has not given up on their efforts to find a technological solution, they believe that an equally important task is to raise parental and caretaker awareness. They have teamed up with Safe Kids USA and forty other organizations to increase parent awareness of the dangers of leaving a child alone in a car. One suggestion is that parents leave something with the infant that they will need in the store—like a purse or cell phone—to remind them of what else they left behind.

But Janette Fennel, founder of Kids and Cars, is still pushing hard for a technology remedy. In an article called "Driven to Make Cars Safe for Kids" in *USA Today*, she said, "If we leave our headlights on, or our keys in the ignition, we get a buzz. Somehow we have decided that it is more important not to have a dead car battery than a dead baby."

Baby-Proofing Your Home

Whenever holidays are approaching, my wife and I begin preparing for when our young grandchildren and grandnieces come to visit. We go from room to room, to ensure there is nothing dangerous that a crawling, or toddling, or curious young child could get into.

Infants and toddlers are amazingly fast when they want to explore something, so it is really important to keep potentially harmful things out of their reach. This is particularly true for "attractive nuisances"—liquids and solids that infants are drawn to because of their color or smell, or both. But attractive nuisances also include things that can be easily knocked over and broken.

We usually start in the kitchen, where many of our cleaning materials—liquid soap, scouring powder, etc.—are kept in the cabinets under the sink. A toddler can easily open these doors, so we empty these cabinets of any and all materials he or she might get into. These are the only cabinets at floor level, so we fill them with light pots and pans and plastic containers that the children can take out and use for play.

Paper and plastic bags, however, should always be stored in out-of-reach containers. Early on, my wife taught me to always keep the handles of the pots and pans facing the counters and never extending out past the front edge of the stove when I am cooking. Particularly when young children are about, and you have to move quickly, it is all too easy to brush against a pot or pan handle that is sticking out and knock the contents onto the floor. Common sense, to be sure, but an important safeguard.

We next move to the living room. As in the kitchen, we ensure that there are caps on all the wall outlets and that any lamp cords are not accessible. Perhaps the greatest danger for little ones in the living room, and dining room, are the sharp corners of the furniture that children can bump into. We have only a few sharp corners on a chest we use as a coffee table so we put cushioned corner guards on these. We also remove anything that can be easily knocked over and broken.

Then we go to the guest bathroom, the only one accessible to our young visitors. In the bathroom, we simply put child-proof latches on the under-sink cabinets. We also use a child-proof wastebasket, one with a lid, to prevent the baby from knocking it over and exploring the contents.

All this may sound like overkill, but it is always better to be safe than sorry. We love having our grandchildren and grand-nieces stay with us, and we don't want to have to worry about them getting into something dangerous if we are not watching.

In this regard, I should also say that we have a big box of wooden blocks, lots of plush and pull toys, and loads of picture books for them to look at and play with that help keep them out of trouble. We also have a limited set of DVDs that they can watch when they are tired and ready for a nap. Keeping the house safe, and having many things for the children to play with and enjoy, make for a (relatively) stress-free and happy holiday for everyone.

Baby Teeth

The emergence of baby teeth is a very individual matter. There is no set timetable for when a baby's new teeth will erupt, how long the process will take, or how painful an experience it will be. Averaged out, the first tooth usually appears during the seventh month, but it can appear months earlier or later.

The pattern of eruption varies as well. In some infants, you can see the bump in the gums for weeks before the tooth itself appears. In other children, the tooth just seems to pop out with no hint of its having been there. The signs that an infant is in the process of teething are as variable as the timing, and can range from irritability and drooling to a skin rash and a low-grade fever. Any out-of-the-ordinary behavior on the part of the infant could be a sign of tooth eruption.

There are a number of things that you can do to ease your baby's teething discomfort. Before using any of them you are well advised to speak to your pediatrician to ensure that you have made the right diagnosis and to hear his or her sugges-tions. As with so many other facets of teething, what works for one child may not work for another. Teething rings that give the infant something hard to bite on help some children; a parent's finger can also serve this purpose. Being given a bottle or a cup of cold water helps some children.

Chilled foods like yogurt, applesauce, or sliced peaches can also have a soothing effect. If none of these remedies work, you might (after consulting with your pediatrician) give your infant a baby Tylenol. Since every infant is different, you really have to experiment to find out what works best for your baby.

Teething does come to an end. A baby usually has a full set of twenty primary teeth by the age of two or three. These baby teeth usually fall out by the age of six or seven. They are gradually replaced by the full complement of thirty-two perma-nent teeth. As with their appearance, the disappearance of the primary teeth is a highly individual matter, and some children keep the last of their primary teeth until the age of twelve. The kind tooth fairy, who leaves your child a gift under the pillow in return for a baby tooth, is, of course, always a welcome and appreciated visitor.

Back-to-School Blues

To paraphrase Shakespeare, some children are born liking school, some children learn to like school, and some children have school thrust upon them (like the young man who told me that the best thing about school was lunch). Another way of saying this is that some children have a harder time getting ready to go back to school than others.

For all children, going back to school is a transition and, like all major transitions, it presents at least a few challenges. These can include a new teacher, a new building, and a new class of children. If the child has to deal with any or all of these challenges, it really helps if you do some preparatory work. The most effective action is to make an appointment to bring the child to meet the teacher in his or her classroom before school starts. This can alleviate some of the child's anxiety about what his or new environment is going to be like.

There are other things that can help prepare children for school as well. Shopping for school clothing and school materials is one way of easing the child back into the schooling frame of mind. During the summer your child might have gotten used to staying up late and sleeping in. Starting a school-year sleep and wake time schedule is another important way of easing the transition.

In some schools, teachers may give reading and math assignments to do over the summer. I am not sure about this practice. On the one hand, it may help the child maintain his or her skill level. But if takes away from the freedom from school work, which is the major blessing of the summer holiday, it might do more harm than good. Again, this is an individual matter. Children who love school may relish the summer work while those who have it thrust upon them will see it as an unnecessary burden.

The transition from half-day kindergarten to full-day first grade is often a major, and difficult, one. All of the suggested stress-reducing tactics mentioned above are particularly important when a child is making that sort of major life change. But now that many kindergartens are full day, and often like watered-down first grade, there is no longer a stark difference between the two levels, and the transition is not such a major change.

For children attending full-day kindergarten, however, the cure is often worse than the disease. This is true because if the child has not learned his or her letters or numbers by the end of the year, retention is often the result. So the child has, at least in his or her mind, failed kindergarten.

How the child deals with returning to school is always an individual matter; some children will welcome it and others dread it. As parents, we need to tailor our school readiness activities to each child's personal attitudes toward entering or returning to school.

Backpacks, The Burden Of

When I visit schools I am often troubled by the number of children I see who appear to be bent over with the weight of the backpack on their shoulders. It is not only at schools—I also see heavy backpacks on children at airports, traveling with their family on a vacation or to visit relatives.

Apparently, I am not alone in my concern. The Academy of Orthopedic Surgeons claims that overloaded backpacks place undue stress on the spine and shoulders, and result in muscle fatigue and strain. The Academy recommends that a child's backpack not exceed 15–20 percent of the child's weight. For example, a child who weighs 80 pounds should not be carrying more than 12–16 pounds in his or her backpack. This is a modal number and should be adjusted according to the child's strength and fitness level.

To avoid injury, the Academy recommends:

- Selecting a backpack that has wide padded straps and a padded back
- Using a hip strap in addition to the back straps when the pack is overloaded
- Making sure that both back straps are tight and are just above the waist
- Making it a rule to place heavier items closest to the child's back
- Teaching the child to use proper lifting techniques, that is, bending at the knees and using the legs to lift the backpack, placing one shoulder strap on at a time
- Encouraging the child to make frequent trips to his or her locker to lighten the load whenever possible
- Having your child use a backpack with wheels (This is a viable option, but peers might look down on it, and that should be considered. Embarrassment might be worse than the pain.)

The Academy suggests that parents look for the following signs that the backpack is too heavy:

- Change in posture while wearing the pack
- Complaints of pain while wearing the pack

- Struggling when putting the pack on or taking it off
- Redness in the shoulders
- Tingling or numbness in arms or shoulders

Backpacks are useful devices and, I suspect, better orthopedically than the heavy briefcases we used to carry with one arm. If backpacks are purchased with care, and if parents follow the Academy's recommendations, backpacks can be a healthy, as well as expedient, way of carrying both books and traveling gear.

Bad Seed, The Proverbial

This topic was prompted by a grandmother who witnessed a boy making repeated surreptitious attempts to taunt and upset her seventeen-month-old granddaughter in the play area of a mall. The grandmother wanted to know whether this behavior was normal.

Embedded in this grandmother's question is a deeper one, namely, Are some children evil by nature, the so-called bad seeds? Disentangling what comes from nature and what from nurture is perhaps most difficult when it comes to psychological traits. Indeed, there is a long-standing controversy over this issue.

The Puritans, for example, believed that children were born with original sin and that, as Puritan minister Cotton Mather solemnly intoned, "You are never too young to go to hell." On other hand, social philosopher Jean-Jacques Rousseau wrote that "Everything is good as it comes from the hands of the maker of the world, but degenerates once it gets into the hands of man." Likewise, Maria Montessori believed that there are no bad children, just bad upbringings and/or education.

Some years ago, criminal behavior was linked to chromosomal anomalies, but additional research has failed to find any consistent connections between such abnormalities and violent and antisocial behavior. (It is also important to say that some chromosomal abnormalities are not genetic and can occur after conception.) So up to this point, there is no clear genetic determinant of aberrant behavior.

My own clinical experience tends to support the views of Rousseau and Montessori. Over four decades of working with troubled children, I have never dealt with one who did not come from a troubled family. My guess is that the young boy about whom the grandmother wrote has been mistreated at home, either by parents or by siblings. Young children are great imitators, and this boy's behavior was learned, not inborn. At the same time, it is also true that while every troubled child comes from a troubled family, not all troubled families produce troubled children. Some young people are extraordinarily resilient and use adversity to strengthen their resolve to overcome it. The success of such children, who overcome extreme adversity, can indeed be attributed to nature.

Bad Theories, Bad Effects

Disney's 2009 refunds for Baby Einstein videos brought to mind a number of current and past cases when wrong or unproven child-rearing theories have done more harm than good. For example, the educational value of Baby Einstein videos is questionable, but the potential harm to infants of watching too much TV is well established.

Other current controversies have to do with the role of vaccinations on the incidence of autism and other illnesses. While vaccinations may do harm to some predisposed children, the benefits of polio, smallpox, and measles vaccines to millions of children can hardly be doubted. Likewise, a connection between ingesting red food dyes and hyperactivity has never been factually supported.

One of the most damaging theories was famed psychologist Bruno Bettelheim's explanation of the causes of autism. He argued persuasively that autism was a syndrome that was produced by what he called "Icebox Mothers." Such mothers, he claimed, through aloofness and lack of warmth, forced their children to withdraw from social contact in order to protect themselves from the pain of future social rejection.

This theory created great anguish and suffering among the parents of such children, who then blamed themselves for their children's condition. Fortunately, we now know that autism has to do with brain functioning and not with child rearing.

Perhaps Sigmund Freud propounded the most egregious error of this kind. In his first theory of neurosis, he contended that the reason his adult patients suffered from anxiety, non-neurological paralysis, and phobias was that they had been sexually molested as children.

For a number of reasons, not the least of which was the revulsion this idea created in the staid Victorian era, Freud decided to give up the theory of sexual abuse as the cause of neurosis. Instead he offered a new theory, that of infantile sexuality. He described the sexual drive as moving through the oral, anal, and genital zones of the body. When the sex drive reached the genital area, around the age of four or five, the child fell in love with the parent of the opposite sex and wanted to be rid of the same-sex parent—the Oedipus and Electra complexes. From this new perspective, Freud argued that the descriptions of childhood sexual abuse given by his adult patients were really what he called "screen memories," memories created to repress the young child's unacceptable wishes to be rid of the same-sex parent.

For more than forty years, the concept of screen memories kept therapists from accepting their patient's descriptions of child abuse as legitimate. It was only in the 1960s, with the factually supported cases of child battering, that the reality of child abuse became a generally accepted, if highly frightening, reality. But for all too many years, reports of child abuse were simply taken as fictions, the creations of infantile sexuality and screen memories.

Sound theories of child behavior can do much good, but bad theories can do a lot of harm.

Bad Words, When Children Use

I recall playing the board game Operation with my then eight-year-old granddaughter, who was visiting us. The game involves trying to remove—with tweezers—tiny loose body parts from small holes. If you touch the edge of a hole with the tweezers, a buzzer goes off to tell you that you have lost that move.

I was intent on removing a kidney when my tweezers touched and the buzzer went off. Although I don't swear very often, I let out a low "Oh sh! . . ." My granddaughter giggled, and I apologized for using a bad word.

I am sure that I am not the only grandparent or parent who has had a similar experience. My granddaughter was old enough to understand both that it was not a nice word and that it was a word she had never heard me use before.

But preschool children are a different story. Age makes an important difference. A two-year-old hearing that word might repeat it without understanding it. And children are more likely to hear these words today either through the media or from other children in preschool centers. If your young child happens to use a swear word and you get visibly upset, you will only encourage its use. A basic rule in dealing with bad words used by children three years and younger is to ignore it if you don't want to reinforce it.

Older children, four or five years old, have a better understanding of the fact that swear words are not socially acceptable. At this age level, children will use these words if they get a rise out of us. They are small and we are big, and they are trying to get control of their world, including us. If we react negatively, they are, in effect, controlling our behavior.

One way to handle this is to say that you do not like to hear such words, that they make you unhappy, so please don't use them when you are around. This type of response reflects a basic principle in dealing with unacceptable language, namely, making rules you can enforce. There is no way to prevent your child from using bad words when he or she is with friends or at places where you cannot hear the conversation. To tell the child never to use the word is making a rule that you cannot enforce, and your child knows it. By making such rules, you weaken your authority and your child's respect for the rules you do make.

We also need to help children appreciate that swear words are sometimes ways of dealing with strong emotions and that it is far better to use them than it is to take aggressive actions. We are human, and there are exceptions to every rule. As I explained to my granddaughter, I used that word because I was upset, but that I was sorry that I made her listen to a bad word. It is okay for our children and grandchildren to learn that we are only human after all.

Bathtub Safety

Our intuitions about what is safe and what is not are often determined by perceptions rather than by facts. We are, for example, generally more fearful about flying in airplanes than about driving in our cars. But the data show that the likelihood of a car accident is much greater than the likelihood of a plane crash. Some of our intuitions about child safety are also not supported by the facts. When bathing our young children, for example, we take particular care to ensure that the water is neither too cold nor too hot. In fact, however, the majority of bathtub injuries are due to slips and falls, not burning or submersion.

Parents are not unique in this regard—researchers have also focused mainly on burns and submersions in their surveys of bathtub injuries. An article called "Tub Thumping: 43,000 Kids Slip in the Bath" recently published in *Pediatrics* and summarized in *Contemporary Pediatrics*, reports the first nationwide study that looks at data regarding bathtub slips and falls. The data for the study came from the National Electronic Survey of the US Consumer Products Commission from 1990 to 2007. The investigators reviewed about 790,000 reports of bathtub and shower injuries, to children and adolescents, who were treated in US emergency rooms over the eighteen-year period.

These figures suggest that there were around 43,000 injuries of this kind in each of the years of the study. This figure indicates that the bathtub injury rate is 5.5 percent per ten thousand young people each year. More than half of the injuries were to children four years old and younger. Most of the injuries, more than 80 percent, were due to slips and falls. The face was the most frequently injured part of the body (48 percent) and injuries to both face and neck were the next most frequent (15 percent).

These results suggest that parents need to be as thoughtful about slips and falls as about temperature. Because parents may not always be able to catch a child who is slipping or falling, rubber mats should be placed on the tub floor to prevent such accidents. Although it is probably unnecessary to say, it is also important not to leave young children alone in the tub. Putting a mat on the bottom of the tub each time the child takes a bath and removing it to dry may seem like a pain. But it is the best insurance against all-too-common bathtub injuries.

Big Events, Children At

One Memorial Day weekend we went to the Hudson Valley to attend our niece's graduation from Marist College. Marist sits right on the bank of the Hudson and has beautiful views across the river to the magnificent Catskill Mountains. It was a warm, sunny day, and the ceremony was to be held on a huge quad sloping down to the river. When we arrived at the college, our niece's three daughters were there to greet us. Stella Blue was five, Raven was three, and Willow was just one.

In most cases, ceremonies like this are really not for little children. At my university, Tufts, for example, there is a tiny quad, chairs are close together, and there is very little room in the aisles. Young children are full of energy and very active; there is just no room for them to run around at most graduations.

But the situation at Marist was different. We were at the top of a huge, sloping quad, the chairs were far apart, and there was plenty of grassy space for the kids to run around in and even for rolling down the gentle hill. So they kept themselves busy throughout the ceremony. This good behavior was aided and abetted by our niece's husband, who brought along plenty of healthy snacks and water, and who was able to take the kids to the toilet, which was conveniently in the library near where we were sitting. One thing that kept them busy during the reading of the graduates names was the body of a dead bird that had fallen from the roof of the library.

The Marist campus is very spread out, and the college had arranged to have shuttle buses and golf carts take the families of the graduates to and from the parking areas. After the ceremony, my niece, her husband, and the children boarded a golf cart to take them to their car. The children were thrilled as they drove away and we waved good-bye to them.

All of this is to say that the exception proves the rule. In general, young children are really not well suited for long, drawn-out ceremonies such as graduations. This event was special of course, because it was their mother who was graduating. Even so, in a more confining environment, they would have been a handful. Many times we take young children to these events because we think it will be provide them with a lasting memory of what seems so important to us. More often than not, however, we mistake what we think might be significant for young children for what really stays in their memory. I am sure that for Stella Blue, Raven, and perhaps Willow, the most memorable part of the whole event was finding the dead bird and riding to their car in the golf cart.

Birth Date and School Entrance

A recent report from Cambridge Assessment, an organization associated with Cambridge University, has reviewed the literature from 1990 to the present regarding the readiness of British four- and five-year-olds to begin formal schooling. The report concludes that children of this age who were born in the summer may suffer serious stress and anxiety that can damage their educational prospects.

The issue of summer birthdays arises because most kindergartens enroll children in the late summer or fall. Children who have summer birthdays are therefore the youngest children in the kindergarten class. The report suggests that such factors as leaving unfamiliar surroundings, facing separation from parents, and adapting to new routines explains why such children perform less well on assessments of progress than do children born in the fall or the winter.

I believe, however, that this explanation misses the major point about children born in the summer. Most children these days, at least here in the United States, have been in one or the other out-of-home program during the early years of life. Leaving familiar surroundings, separation, and adapting to new routines, therefore, can hardly be the issue. Yet in some of our US communities, as many as 30 percent of kindergarteners are held back or placed in transition classes, and the majority of these children have summer birthdays.

The real problem is that the curriculum is always geared to the oldest children—and is too difficult for most in the younger age group. That is the major reason summer birthday children are often held back or put in transition classes. Changing the entrance age does not help because the curriculum is always adapted to the oldest children.

There are a number of solutions. When I was growing up we had A and B classes. Children born between July and December began school in the fall, and children born between January and June started school in the winter. This reduced the age variation in the classes but was awkward for maintaining given graduation dates and the like. Another solution is to have the kindergarten provide a flexible curriculum geared to children at different developmental levels. This has become less possible now that first grade has become more rigid and requires that children know their numbers and letters for admission.

Perhaps the best solution is multi-age grouping. In this arrangement, five- and six-year-old children, or five-, six-, and seven-year-old children, are grouped together. Children of comparable abilities, regardless of age, can then learn together. In addition, only a third of the class is new to the teacher each year, and he or she can really get to know the children. Moreover, older children can teach the younger children, and in so doing improve their own learning. Some parents object to this arrangement, however, for fear of dumbing down. That is, they believe the older children will not be stimulated enough.

A number of parents who are concerned about the birth date effect hold their summer birthday children back a year. In some communities, this has raised the mean age of the first grade class so that the winter birth date children are the youngest!

Although multi-age grouping is the best solution, it is not likely to be widely adapted. For parents there is no easy answer. If you have a summer birthday child, talk with the kindergarten

teacher and use your own judgment about your child's intellectual and social maturity to decide whether to send him or her
on or hold the child back.

Summer birthday children are too often confronted with
curricula that demand abilities that they have not yet attained.
So make the decision based on the abilities and dispositions of
your child and the flexibility and openness of the classroom he
or she is going into.

Biting

Between the ages of one and three, some children go through
a stage of biting other children. Although this occurs most
frequently in child care centers, it can happen at other times,
such as at birthday parties. Our initial adult interpretation of a
biting incident is that it is an act of aggression—a child is angry
with another child and wants to hurt him or her.

This quite natural assumption is not supported by what we
know of child development. Young children are egocentric;
they are unable to accept another person's point of view when
it is different from their own. That is, a child who is biting
another cannot appreciate what the other child is feeling until
that child cries out. Once a child bites, he or she may discover
that it serves a purpose, making the other child leave the scene
or abandon a toy. In most cases, even a child who continues to
bite does not do so to hurt the other child, but rather to attain
some other goal.

Children bite other children for a variety of reasons. Some
children may bite in order to get the attention of adult caregivers. Other children may bite because they have seen other

children bite and are simply imitating them. Most often children bite other children because of stress or frustration. Young children have few means of expressing their feelings, and biting is one of the few they have for venting their anger and resentment. In most cases, the victim is not the cause of the child's unhappiness—he or she just happens to be the available target. Nonetheless, biting is upsetting to the parents of the victim, particularly if the bite breaks the skin, causes bleeding, or leaves bite marks.

In order to deal effectively with a child who bites, you must first try to determine the cause. Does the biting usually occur over the use of a toy? Or when the child is hungry and tired or otherwise frustrated? Or does it only occur when a particular other child is present? Sometimes biting coincides with a change in the child's life, such as the birth of sibling, a move to a new house and neighborhood, a divorce, or simply attending a new child care center.

If biting occurs over a toy, making more toys available may solve the problem. When it is another child who seems to provoke biting, it is best just to keep them apart. For children who bite when they are tired and hungry, having desirable snacks ready when out shopping or doing errands may help solve the problem. When biting is in response to a change in life circumstances, extra care needs to be taken to reassure the child of parental love and that he or she is not being abandoned or rejected.

If a biting incident occurs, it is important to remain calm and to remember that the situation is a frightening one for both children. The child who is bitten should be attended to first with whatever first aid is required. Then both children need to be given hugs and reassurance that everything is all right and no serious damage has been done. Parental feelings are more problematic. The parents of a child who has been bitten may be quite upset and need reassurance that the biting was not intentional and that every effort will be made so that it will not happen again.

In most cases, biting disappears as the child acquires more effective coping skills. You can help your child in this regard by rewarding and praising the child's efforts at engaging in positive social interactions.

Brain, The Moral

Are empathy and morality learned or hard-wired in children? A recent University of Chicago study sought to answer this question. Seventeen seven- to twelve-year-old children were the subjects of the study. The children were wired for an MRI brain scan and shown pictures of people experiencing pain produced either accidentally or intentionally. The researchers found that when the children observed people who were in pain due to accidental causes, the pain centers in the brain were activated. But when the children were shown pictures of people who were intentionally hurt, the brain centers dealing with social interaction and morality were activated. The investigators suggested that their findings indicate that empathy and morality may be hard-wired in the brain.

While these results are interesting, they fail to take into account the developmental and experiential dimensions. A number of years ago, Jean Piaget made an extensive study of the development of morality in children. He used a variety of techniques.

Perhaps the most powerful was the one in which he presented children with two child accident scenarios and asked them to say which child was more to blame and which one should be punished the most. In one scenario, a child broke six dishes while helping his mother put them away. In the other scenario, a child broke one dish in an effort to get some candy that he was told not to take.

Piaget found that before the age of six or seven, children judged guilt in terms of the amount of damage done, rather than on the basis of intentionality. That is, young children said that the child who broke the most dishes was more to blame and should be punished more. After the age of six or seven, children judged culpability based on the child's intentions and not on the amount of damage.

In a follow up study, my students and I included stories of intentional and unintentional personal injury (an accidental bloody nose as opposed to the result of a punch by another child). We found the shift at the same ages as Piaget, with the exception that children arrived at intentionality a year or so earlier when it had to do with personal injury rather than property damage.

The point is, while some aspects of empathy and morality may be hard-wired, at least some aspects are also related to experience and development.

C

Chores for Tots

We usually think of chores as only appropriate for school-age children. But even young children can benefit from doing needed tasks around the house. For young children to benefit from chores, however, three conditions have to be met. First, the chores themselves have to be within the child's range of abilities. Second, the chores should be meaningful and not just busywork. Third, chores should be presented as options for the child and not as requirements.

Preschoolers are very much into initiative and getting things done on their own. But they also like to feel like they are part of the family and doing useful things to help out. Meaningful chores build on this motivation, and children will engage in them without the promise of reward. Asking young children to perform simple household chores is not engaging in exploitation or demanding slave labor. It is one of the best ways for young children to learn many important social skills and habits.

Young children might be asked to empty waste baskets, help sort and fold freshly laundered clothes, feed and water pets, water plants, and help make their beds. These activities reinforce children's sense of being a respected and contributing family member. Asking young children to do chores should be in the tone of cooperation: "I could really use some help in making this bed, or in sorting these clothes." And praise should be for the effort put in, not the result: "Thank you—that was really a big help. You are really a good worker."

Doing chores has both immediate and long-term benefits. The immediate benefits are the sense of accomplishment and good humor that children get from feeling that they are working members of the family. The long-term benefits were described in a University of Minnesota study. The investigators reported that the best predictor of a young adult's success in his or her twenties was having performed household chores at ages three and four. The measures of success were completing education, starting a career path, IQ scores, and positive relationships with family and friends. The same results were not found for young adults who did not do household chores until they reached adolescence. These results suggest that there are many benefits from having young children participate in household chores.

There is, as always, a caution. As parents, we have to be careful not to demand too much or to be overly concerned with how well the task was performed. Even if a bed is not made well, and a toy or two is not picked up, the important point is that the child worked at the chore. We shouldn't expect perfection from young children, but we should honestly value and appreciate their efforts.

Communication with Children, Good

As a teenager I dated a girl who always said, "Grind me up a pound" whenever I shifted gears in my old rattletrap of a car. I am sure she thought she was being clever, but this language habit really turned me off.

Without really thinking about it, we can get into language habits with our children which may not only annoy them but give them mixed messages as to what we are trying to communicate. While the mixed message may be entirely in the language, it sometimes occurs because our behavior contradicts our words. A few examples may help illustrate the kind of double messages I have in mind.

One of the most frequent language habits is the one of saying "okay?" after we give a direction or a command. If we say, "We are going to bed now, okay?" we are, in effect giving our child a choice as to whether or not to accept our invitation. We shouldn't be annoyed if the child decides he or she does not want to go to bed. Another example is, "We gotta go now, okay?" If our child does not seem to be in any hurry to get ready, it is because it sounds as if we are giving him or her the option to go or to stay. If we become conscious of such language habits, it is easy to break them.

Another common verbal habit is to use the word "nice" vaguely, as in "That isn't nice." "Nice" is a wishy-washy word that doesn't mean much to kids. When my granddaughter was two and she was picking her nose, I made a face and said, "Gross, Heather." At six, she still teases me by putting her finger to her nose to get my reaction. We need to use words which are clear and get our message across. Another wishy-washy word to avoid is "good," as in "Don't do that—be good," when we mean "Stop teasing your brother." The more specific and exact we are with our words, the better chance we have of getting our message across.

The other form of missed communication comes from not matching our body language with our words. If something frightening happens and alarms us, like an unexpected flash of lightning, it doesn't really help our child if we say, "Don't be scared!" It is much more honest and reassuring to a child if we say something like, "That was really scary, wasn't it." Likewise, if we are taking our child to meet a new babysitter or preschool teacher, it doesn't help him or her if we say, "Relax, honey, its okay," when we ourselves are a bit tense and on edge. If we say, "It sometimes is a little scary when we meet new people," we match our body language to our words.

The words we use with young children are important not only for being clear in what we wish to communicate but also in giving children a model of meaningful language usage.

Computer, Child-Proofing The

Two-year-old Willow was one of the grandnieces we had visiting with us over a Fourth of July weekend. She reminded us of how important it was to baby-proof the house for this age child. She is very fast and very clever. Although we had been conditioned to shut all the doors so she could not wander, by the end of the week she figured out how to work the latches. Once I happened to keep her from closing the door on her fingers. And one evening I let her put the cup-full of kibble into the dog's dish. The next day, when she was out of sight for a moment, she got into the large crock where we keep the kibble.

When I found her, she had filled not only his food dish, but also his water dish, and was in the process of tossing measuring cups of kibble around the kitchen.

Our new technologies have added a new domain of child-proofing. This domain was highlighted by a recent research article published in the *Journal of Preventive Medicine*. The researchers found that over the period from 1994 to 2006 there was a seven-fold increase in the number of emergency room admissions for computer related injuries. Children under five were found to be most at risk. Most frequently, the injuries were caused by the young child's tripping over computer cables. In so doing they can easily bump their heads on sharp corners. Although this cause of accidents sounds counterintuitive, consider the fact that the most frequent cause of death in young children is swallowing balloons.

The chief researcher of the study, Lara McKenzie, listed a number of precautions to be taken to prevent computer-related injuries in young children. The most important is to keep computers on solid, stable furniture, away from sharp edges, and unreachable to small children. It is also important to separate the children's play areas from those areas where there are computers. In setting up the computer, all of the cables should be gathered and secured either with tape or with materials made specifically for that purpose. Other common-sense precautions include keeping the computer against a wall and away from walkways. Finally, McKenzie advised parents not to allow young children access to computers unless there is adult supervision of the activity.

If all of this seems like overkill, it is not. As I learned from watching Willow run out the door, climb on anything climbable, and eat anything she could grab, children at this stage have enormous curiosity and few learned fears. That is a very dangerous combination. For this age group, we should take the trouble to make the environment safe, rather than be sorry that we didn't.

Computers and Preschoolers

There is considerable debate among educators, child psychologists, and pediatricians regarding the value of computer use by young children. Some stress that computers are now part of our world and that an early introduction to them has a variety of benefits, including improved cognitive and social skills, as well as solid preparation for more advanced computer use. Others argue that children need to learn about the real world before they learn about the virtual one, and that too-early computer use may damage the young child's still maturing sensory and motor abilities.

What makes deciding which way to go difficult is having so little good research on the topic. What we do know for sure is that computer use has been increasing at least for five-year-olds. A report by the US Department of Education called "Computer and Internet Use by Children and Adolescents in 2001" found that about 75 percent of five-year-olds were using computers. In a 2004 survey study, "Early Childhood Computer Experience and Cognitive and Motor Development," the investigators found that rural young children were as involved with computers as were there suburban and urban age-mates. They also found that girls used computers as frequently as boys. These data suggest that computers may be breaking down some previous cultural and gender divides.

There also seems to be some agreement that computers *not* be introduced before the age of three. Even those who argue for computer use after the age of three offer a number of cautions: the programs have to be age-appropriate, for example, more animation than text; the time spent on computers should be limited; the physical arrangement should be comfortable for the child; and type sizes should be large so that young children do not have to strain their eyes. Many young children seem to take naturally to computers, while others do not. These preferences should be respected, and a child should never be forced into computer use.

My own sense is that children can learn to use computers more competently and effectively after the age of seven or eight. If young children get over-involved in computer use, they may learn habits—thanks to their limited motor and mental abilities—that they may have to unlearn later. I recognize, of course, that the pervasiveness of computers at home and preschool makes young children's experimentation with this technology inevitable. As long as their experimentation is game playing, and respectful of the cautions mentioned above, it is unlikely to do any harm.

Where the harm comes in is using computers to give preschoolers a head start on academics or to keep them occupied while parents are doing something else. Computers are here to stay and are part of our environment. The same is true of microwave ovens, but we don't use the fact of their pervasiveness to justify letting young children use them. The point is, the pervasiveness of a technology is no guarantee of its appropriateness for unlimited use by young children.

Coping Skills, Teaching and Modeling

A few years ago we spent our Christmas holiday with my wife's family in the Hudson Valley. At the end of the visit, our grandniece Stella Blue was distressed to see us, especially my wife, prepare to leave. While holding back tears, she seemed to think for a moment, and then asked my wife, "What is the ocean like in winter?" She has spent a week or so with us on Cape Cod every summer since she was a baby and loves it there. My wife answered that the ocean gets very rough in the winter.

The change of subject helped Stella Blue deal with her distress. She had learned a coping skill from her grandmother, who had taught her, "When you are feeling sad, think of something glad." And she did.

Young children can learn simple coping strategies, particularly when they are phrased in rhyme. Indeed, over the centuries children have devised their own coping strategies, which have been passed down from generation to generation. For example, "Sticks and stones will break my bones, but names will never hurt me." And when they are troubled by bad weather they can chant, "Rain, rain, go away, come again another day." And at the end of the school year they can express their pent-up frustrations with, "No more writing no more books, no more teacher's dirty looks!"

Unfortunately, much of this language and lore is being lost because children no longer have the time to engage in the self-initiated play that provided opportunity for modifying and passing on the jokes, games, riddles, and chants that made up the culture of childhood.

That is why it is important to teach even young children to cope with the many different stressful events they will necessarily encounter. For example, a useful rhyme for when children get really upset is, "When you are angry, when you see red, stop, don't hit—count to ten instead."

A common stressor for children is being snubbed or left out of games, parties, or groups. Rejection is difficult to cope with, but it is made a little easier if the child can say in defense, "You are you, and I am me, but I'm the best that I can be. Too bad about you." For older children who are worried about the outcome of an upcoming event, it is a useful strategy to learn to "think of the worst possible thing that could happen. If you can deal with that, then anything better is a gift."

Coping strategies are acquired most easily if we model them for our children. Young people learn best through imitation. How we handle stress is the way our children will learn to deal with it. That is why it is so important that we try to model effective coping strategies for our children.

Count Your Blessings

Some time ago I gave a talk to parents whose children attend a local Montessori school. I usually talk for about an hour and then leave half an hour or so for questions. The questions I received were similar to the ones I hear from parents wherever I speak. One mother was concerned that her son was not diligent enough about his homework and seemed unmotivated. Other parents asked about children who are messy, who neglect their household chores, or won't eat their spinach. In the past, I have tried to give parents some explanations for their children's behavior. I believe that knowing the cause of any behavior is the best guide to knowing how to modify it.

But at this event I answered in a different way. I surprised myself, because it was nothing I had thought about in advance, or planned. It was entirely spontaneous and from the heart.

Afterward, many parents came up to me and thanked me for my answer.

What I told the parents was the following story. Two-and-a-half years ago my son and daughter-in-law finally had the child they had been trying to have for several years. But their daughter, Maya, had Down syndrome. We were all devastated. Our expectation that our new grandchild would be as bright and beautiful as her cousins was crushed.

We all went through a period of mourning for this child who never came. But we have all grown to love and to cherish the child that we do have. We are lucky in that Maya is very healthy and at the top of the scale of ability for children with Down syndrome. She is a warm, loving child who is making remarkable progress thanks to the commitment of her parents and an extensive early intervention program.

She already has good language skills, swims, and rides horseback. She is now enrolled in a regular kindergarten, is reading, and is the love of her classmates and teachers. Yes, she sometimes has accidents and, much less often now, has trouble articulating because of poor muscle control and other problems. But our distress about any negatives is totally eclipsed by our joy in her positive achievements.

I ended this little story by telling the parent who had asked the original question that she should be so happy that she has a child who is able to do homework. Having a child with disabilities makes you realize how lucky you are to have such a youngster who does not.

From my new perspective, I suggested that rather than try to correct what the parent saw as faults, she might want to show her appreciation for all of the positive things her child is and does. Perhaps if we accentuate the positive, the negatives will take care of themselves. In the end, my message was: "If you have a healthy, normal child just count your blessings."

Creative Thinking, Nourishing

The contemporary emphasis in our schools on academic excellence is silencing the natural curiosity, imagination, and creativity of teachers and children. Academic learning rewards children for learning what is already known, it encourages *reproductive* thinking. Such thinking is important; we really don't have to reinvent the wheel. But the over-emphasis on reproductive thinking also leads children to use what is already known as the means to deal with new and unexpected problems. While this may result in a solution, it may not be the best or the most effective solution. Yet education rewards such problem solving with high grades. The educational reward system, in effect, discourages curiosity, imagination, and creativity, or *productive* thinking. And productive thinking is like a muscle—if you don't use it you lose it.

There are a number of game-like activities that we can play with a child (or children) in order to nourish his or her productive thinking abilities. One of these is the Multiple Uses game. In this game you ask the child to think of as many uses as he or she can for familiar household items like rubber bands, paper plates, or sponges. This encourages the child to think beyond the familiar uses of the objects and to create new ones. A variant of the Multiple Uses game is the Multiple Names game. In this game we ask the child to make up new names for familiar objects like a chair, a toothbrush, or a comb. These can be funny, but they also help the child not to let names limit the way they think about the objects named.

Another game can be played after reading a book or watching a movie or television program. You might ask the child something like, "What do you think might have happened if they hadn't found the treasure, or they hadn't caught the thief?" This game helps children understand that the same series of events can have different outcomes. A variant of this game is to have the child make up a story about the family pet, or about the family house or car. While the starting point might be a real event, the child needs to be challenged to go further and to add his or her own made-up events.

When out of doors on a nice day, a challenging game is to ask the child to look up into the sky and to see if they can recognize any familiar shapes in the clouds. Because the clouds are changing, this can be an ongoing game: "Oh, now it looks like a. . . . " This and the other activities described above help the child to go beyond what is known and what is certain and to explore the possible and the imaginable.

Playing games such as these with your child will help counteract the reproductive thinking emphasis that has become all too common in our schools.

Crying, Decoding Infant

A problem for many parents of young infants is the baby who cries fitfully for no apparent reason. The baby may have had a full meal at the breast or bottle, slept a little while, and then resumed crying on and off for hours. Picking up and cuddling the baby quiets him or her for a brief period of time, but then the crying erupts again. The parents check to see if the diaper needs to be changed, and it doesn't. The baby has just been to the pediatrician and was given a clean bill of health.

At this point, after being up for long hours, parents wonder, "What does the baby want?" A very intuitive answer, given that all else is in order, is that the baby is hungry and wants to be fed again. But after a few sucks, the baby shows no more interest and starts crying again.

One strong possibility—and this was suggested by Freud—is that the infant has an urge to suck but the urge is quite unrelated to food; sucking is pleasurable in itself. That would explain why the infant is not interested in the breast or bottle; he or she is not interested in food, just sucking. This is where the pacifier comes in. For many infants in this situation, the pacifier solves the problem by giving the infant a release for its urge to suck.

Parents worry, however, that the baby will become addicted to the pacifier and be reluctant to give it up. But in most cases the infant will lose interest in the pacifier on his or her own once the urge to suck declines. This usually happens toward the second half of the first year. Once the infant shows signs of losing interest, the pacifier should be withdrawn gradually. If the baby still seems to need it, it can be given back temporarily but withdrawn again when the baby again shows signs of lack of interest in it.

It should be said, however, that the pacifier can be seductive. Parents may be tempted to let the infant continue to use the pacifier after the baby gives every sign of not needing it any longer. This is misuse of the pacifier, which may indeed cause it to be habit forming. The infant may come to look upon it as an all-purpose tension reducer. This is not healthy for the infant, who should be learning more adaptive methods for dealing with stress.

The important point, and one that holds true for all facets of child rearing, is that you have to pay attention to what the baby does. Through his or her cries and actions, the baby communicates fears, likes, dislikes, and needs. If we take our cues from the infant, as when he or she shows signs of no longer needing a pacifier, we will not go too far wrong. Indeed, watching your baby closely is the best way of decoding his or her behavior.

D

Day Care Centers

Day care centers, which decades ago were looked down upon and disdained as being for children of destitute and indigent mothers, are now regarded as essential for two-parent and single-parent working families. Day care centers now look after more than 30 percent of US children under the age of five.

Contemporary day care centers serve parents at all socioeconomic levels. They range from those providing bare-bones child care to those that offer the latest educational innovations, music, foreign language, and ballet lessons together with field trips to museums, zoos, and aquariums.

Most qualified day care centers have some positive features for young children. They often offer a number areas for pursuing different interests: one for block play, a sand table, a quiet corner for listening to stories or music, and hopefully an easily accessible outdoor area for activities involving the large muscles such as going down slides and riding tricycles.

Of course there are some disadvantages as well. One is that children are more likely to get sick in a child care setting than in a more expensive setting with fewer children and more teachers. Because the child-to-teacher ratio is often higher in a day care center than, say, in a Montessori school, a child is also likely to get less individual attention. Day care center hours also tend to be inflexible, and there may be special charges for early drop-offs and late pick-ups. Finally, because staff turnover tends to happen at a higher rate (largely due to low pay), children may have to adjust to a number of different caregivers over the course of his or her attendance.

In choosing a day care facility, you have to be clear about your priorities. What is most important—cost, closeness to your home, facilities, or educational programs? Once you have established your priorities, you can locate referral agencies that have a list of day care facilities within your community. One way to shorten your list is to look for those centers which are accredited either by the National Association for the Education of Young Children or by the National Association for Family Child Care. This will ensure that the center has met minimum standards for safety, sanitation, teacher qualification, and basic facilities, toys, and equipment.

Visit several centers and get feel for the facility and the staff. If possible visit the center while it is in session to get a sense of what the experience would be like for your child. Once you have made your choice, keep in mind that it is not written in stone. If you or your child is unhappy with the center (unless it is simply a matter of separation anxiety), you can always find another. The most important factor influencing your decision should be that you feel comfortable and assured that your child is in a safe, clean, well-outfitted setting and looked after by trained, competent caregivers and educators.

Death, Talking with Young Children About

While the motorcade carried John F. Kennedy's casket to the cemetery, cameras switched to the preschool-age John-John, looking on and saluting the flag-draped caisson. After the family returned to the White House, however, John-John went immediately to the Oval Office in search of his father.

When my son Rick was four, we found a dead bird in our yard. I put it in a plastic bag and told him that we were going to bury it. He asked me why I didn't just put it in the trash can. Puzzled, I asked him why we should do that. Without hesitation he said, "It will be easier for him to get out of the trash can."

Young children do not understand the concept of death. Life and death are biological concepts that also presuppose an understanding of life processes that most children do not acquire until the age of eight or nine. At that age, they go through a brief period of anxiety when they are shocked to learn that their parents, like all living things, are mortal. So the question becomes one of what to say to a young child who has lost a relative, friend, or pet to whom he or she was attached. Knowing what not to say is at least as important as know what to say. For example, it is best to avoid giving explanations. If you say, "Grandpa died because he was sick," the child can take this to mean that everyone who gets sick dies and then worry about getting sick and dying. If you say something like, "God took him because he was so good," the child may take this as invitation to be bad.

It is best to be factual and supportive, saying something like, "Grandpa died, and we won't ever see him again, but we loved him very much and he loved us." Although young children do not mourn the loss of a beloved person at the time of his or death, this does not mean that the mourning will never occur. It is just delayed—usually until adolescence, when young people attain new mental abilities that allow them to reconstruct their personal history. Adolescents who lost a parent at an early age, for example, may try and imagine some of things they might have done with the parent had he or she lived.

As humans, we are blessed or cursed with the ability to foresee our own demise. If we approach the idea of death in a factual and caring way with young children, we provide them with the best preparation for their eventual acceptance of the reality of death.

Developmental Differences

During the question-and-answer period following one of my lectures, a mother said that she was troubled that her baby was not walking when her friend's baby, of equal age, was already doing so. This mother's concern highlights a common worry, particularly among first-time mothers. What parents need to remember is that we are biological beings whose rate of growth is determined largely by our heredity. Puberty is perhaps the best example because it is so obvious. Some young people attain puberty (including sexual maturation and growth spurts in height and weight) at eleven, some at twelve, some at thirteen, some at fourteen, and some even later. All adolescents attain puberty, but they get there at different rates.

A healthy baby will crawl, walk, and talk when their biological clock tells the baby that he or she has the muscle power and motor control to do so. In addition, it is important to recognize that some babies focus on talking to the exclusion of walking while the reverse is true for other infants. Most babies bring these two facets of their development into line on their own, without special help or training.

This mother's comment illustrates another caution that needs to be emphasized, namely, the risk of comparisons. We all want our children to do well, but the only measures of how well they are doing are developmental norms such as those offered in most child development manuals. Although such markers of development are useful, they are just averages, and they fail to convey the normal range of variation for achievements such as crawling, talking, and walking. And this normal range of variation can be a few months on either side of the modal age. So the normative ages must be taken as suggestions only.

Most importantly, for healthy babies, these age-of-attainment variations are no longer apparent by the time the children are three or four. The analogy with puberty is again apropos. Once they are into their twenties, it is almost impossible to tell who was a late maturer and who was an early maturer. Comparisons are not only misleading, they are also risky. If we become overly anxious about our child's developmental progress, we may communicate this to the child, who may become equally concerned.

One strategy for turning comparison into a healthy practice is to compare the child with himself of herself. On our garden shed, we mark our granddaughter Lily's height every time she comes to visit. Children love such markers of their progress, and we should use these in our evaluation of the child.

Attending to, and commenting, upon a child's own progress keeps us focused on our own child and avoids harmful comparisons. It also helps to teach the child to compete with himself or herself while encouraging cooperation with others.

Discipline

In the 1960s, Israeli psychologist Haim Ginott published a book called *Between Parent and Child*. He became a popular figure on talk shows, and his book was a best seller. His students Adele Faber and Elaine Maizlish followed up with an even more successful best seller, *How to Talk So Kids Will Listen, and Listen So Kids Will Talk*.

I was reminded of these books when I was at the pier in Hyannis on Cape Cod. A mother and her three small children were walking along the pier, and the youngest—two or three at most—kept going dangerously close to the edge. To dissuade him, his mother said, "Don't go so near the edge. If you fall in, there is big fish in there that will swallow you up."

Faber and Maizlish echoed one of the points that Ginott made, namely, that using fearful consequences to modify a child's behavior doesn't work. It fails because the child either doesn't believe the consequence or takes the parent seriously and becomes frightened. What these authors suggest is that in such situations, you simply leave the field, removing the child from the tempting situation. In the home, if you do not want a young child to climb up the stairs, it makes sense to put up a gate rather than to try and impede the child's impulse with words.

But Ginott also emphasized that the words we use with children are important. He and his students suggest that parents try to respond to the child's feelings rather than trying to use logic. If a child is angry, a parent might say, "I know you are angry and that is okay. I would be too if someone did that to me." Or, if the child is sad or unhappy for some reason, a parent might say, "It seems to me you are very unhappy about something. Do you want to talk about it?" In addition, when correcting children, these author's suggest using "I" rather than "you" messages. Instead of, "You never pick up your dirty clothes," you might say, "It really makes extra work for me when I have to pick up your dirty clothes." This approach helps the child to learn that their actions have consequences rather than making them feel attacked.

Another important point that Ginott makes is that "love is not enough." By this he means that loving a child does not preclude discipline but rather demands it. If we really love a child, then we show this love by helping that child become a responsible social being. We do this not only by setting limits but also by demonstrating with our own behavior the example we would like him or her to follow.

Obviously, the Ginott approach does not always work with all children, but its widespread continued acceptance and use by parents makes clear that this is one of the most effective and child-friendly approaches to child rearing and discipline.

Divorce, Effects upon Children

Divorce is a one-time legal event, but it has long-lasting psychological consequences. The effects of divorce depend upon several interacting factors. Perhaps most important of these are the relationship between the parents, the age of the child, and the child's gender.

The relationship between the parents prior to and after the divorce is the single most important factor in predicting how children will cope. In the best case, the parents decide they are not suited for one another but are united in their love and concern for the children. They minimize the changes in lifestyle and make sure that the children understand that there are two kinds of love. One kind is that between two adults, and that can change. The other kind is that between parents and children, and that never changes. Divorce is never easy on anyone, but if the parents have an amicable relationship, and maintain a close relationship with the children, the impact separation is considerably reduced after the divorce.

At the other end of the spectrum is the divorce in which the parents are angry and bitter. The parents may be so caught up in their own feelings that they fail to take the children's feelings into account. Even more serious is the divorce in which the warring parents use the children as pawns to hurt the other parent. One or both parents may ask the children to take sides or bad-mouth the other parent. This puts the child in a completely untenable position.

Divorce is hard enough on children; it shouldn't be taken by one parent as a license to dump on the other parent. Both parents need to recognize that whatever their differences, the divorce does not alter the fact that they are parents. In front of the children, responsible parents will never say bad things about the other parent, regardless of their personal feelings. A parent is a parent, and children should be given the opportunity to make their own character evaluations.

Age is another important factor. Preschool children do not understand divorce and may see the disappearance of one parent as rejection or abandonment. They need to be reassured that the parents still love them and that they will continue to see both parents (only if this is true, of course.) School-age children are most concerned about what is going to happen to them—change of their living arrangements, school, neighborhood, etc. For this age group, it is critical to sit down with them and to explain in detail if and how living arrangements will change, visitation issues, and so on.

Divorce hits young adolescents perhaps hardest of all. They are at the romantic stage and believe that there is one special person made for them, and when they find that person they fall in love and live happily ever after. The divorce is a blow to their romantic ideal, and their readiness to enter into serious relationships. Parents need to be frank with adolescents about the reasons for the divorce and remind them that many couples do stay together for a lifetime.

The gender of the child is still another factor. Preschool boys, for example, may believe that their wish to have their father leave (the Oedipus complex) caused the divorce. In later years, these young men may become accident prone as a means of dealing with their guilt. Preschool girls may blame their mother for not being attractive enough, and become seductive with men once they reach adolescence. Interestingly, preschool girls who lose their fathers through death are usually shy and inhibited with older boys and men.

To say that divorce poses risks for children is not to say that divorce should be avoided. In many cases it may be the least worst decision. What these considerations do mean is that divorce is as painful for children as it is for parents, if not more so. Despite their own pain, parents must appreciate how much their children need to be talked to about the divorce, reassured about their future, and be given support for their feelings of anger and resentment.

In most cases, it takes families five years, give or take, to fully recover from the divorce. Recovery is much faster and healthier when the divorce is amicable than when it is not.

Dyslexia

Dyslexia is the most common learning disability in children and is primarily (but not entirely) a difficulty in learning to read, write, and spell. Because there are various types and causes of dyslexia, it is hard to determine how common it is. Determining the percentage of people who suffer from dyslexia is made even more difficult by the fact that the disability can range from mild to severe. Some surveys suggest that, if you include the whole spectrum of dyslexic disorders, as many as 20 percent of people in the US experience some facets of this disability.

Although there are several causes of dyslexia, the primary cause (the most common one) is a brain dysfunction. Those with primary dyslexia are rarely able to read beyond the fourth grade level and may continue to have difficulty in reading, spelling, and writing as adults. Recent research using functional magnetic resonance imaging (fMRI) found that when dyslexic children attempted to read, there was little activity in the brain areas that control auditory and language functions. The fMRI data also suggests that dyslexia is primarily an auditory rather than a visual disorder. Language must first be learned through the ears before it can be understood through eyes when it is transposed to the printed page. Primary dyslexia tends to run in families. But even if dyslexia runs in the family, it is necessary to first rule out other possible causes of reading disability before making the diagnosis. It is important to test a child's hearing and vision to ensure that these are not the problem. Once visual and auditory disabilities have been ruled out, there are a number of signs that point to a preschooler with dyslexia. These include:

- Difficulty remembering nursery rhymes and rhyming words, such as cat and hat
- Showing little interest in letters and words, although enjoying stories
- Mixing up directional words like "up" and "down" or "in" and "out"
- Jumbling up letters or words, such as saying "beddy tear" instead of "teddy bear"
- Difficulty arranging blocks or objects according to size
- Physical coordination problems, such as difficulty catching a ball, skipping, or hopping

Recognizing dyslexia early is essential, so that schools can provide special training for the child. Most of this is a combination of auditory, visual, and motor skill training. Although educational programs can help a dyslexic child, it is a life-long disability. Medication is not used in the treatment of dyslexia.

Dyslexia is not limited to any particular racial or ethnic group, nor is it linked to any intellectual limitations. Indeed, many individuals learn strategies to deal with the disability and become quite successful as adults.

E

Ear Infections

Anyone can get an ear infection, but it is, after the common cold, the second most frequent illness in young children. More than three out of four children will have experienced one or more ear infections before their third birthday.

An ear infection is an inflammation of middle ear, the section of the ear just inside the eardrum. Bacteria cause fluid to build up behind the eardrum, and the resulting pressure brings about the inflammation. The pressure on the eardrum is what causes an earache, one of the major symptoms of these infections. Fever often accompanies the pain.

The key culprits in the frequency of ear infections in children are the Eustachian tubes, which connect the throat to the nose and to the middle ear. These tubes help equalize the pressure between the outer ear and middle ear, which are separated by the eardrum. In young children, these tubes are smaller and straighter than they will be later. If a child has a cold or the flu, or other respiration problems, these tubes can become blocked and the fluid from the infection cannot drain.

The familiar ear popping on plane trips is a result of a similar pressure imbalance. It is also the reason that during air travel many infants suffer pain on landings and takeoffs, when pressure changes are the most rapid.

Many ear infections occur before children are able to talk and describe the cause of their distress. For these children, the most common symptoms are:

- Tugging or pulling at the ear
- Fussiness and crying
- Trouble sleeping
- Fever (especially in infants and younger children)
- Fluid draining from the ear
- Clumsiness or problems with balance
- Trouble hearing or responding to soft sounds

For older children, fluid may build up even in the absence of pain, and can cause hearing difficulties. Suspect an ear infection if your child:

- Does not respond to soft sounds
- Turns up the radio or television
- Talks louder
- Is reported to be inattentive at school

If you suspect your child has an ear infection, you should take him or her to the doctor. Many ear infections last only a few days, even without medication. That is why many doctors take a wait and see approach before prescribing medication.

Antibiotics won't help if the ear infection is viral, and they may have side effects. Also, too frequent use of antibiotics can lead to antibiotic-resistant bacteria. For children who have frequent ear infections, however, antibiotics may be in order to prevent further infection.

Instead of or in addition to antibiotics, your doctor may prescribe child-managed dosages of over-the-counter pain medication, such as ibuprofen, acetaminophen, and eardrops. *Do not give your child aspirin if he or she has a fever or other flu-like symptoms.* Aspirin has been found to be a risk factor in Reye's syndrome, a potentially fatal disease that has numerous detrimental effects to many organs, especially the brain and liver.

Like the flu and common cold, ear infections are one of those childhood illnesses that are simply a fact of life for parents of young children.

Education, Preschool

Any educational program is, of necessity, also a child well-being program. This is true even at the college or university level, where the school assumes the role of *in loco parentis*. At whatever level of education, a teacher who is not concerned with the emotional and physical health of his or her students is not worthy of the profession. That said, the issue of student well-being is particularly acute in early childhood. This is true because young children are much more dependent upon and in need of adult care than older children. Indeed, until recently it was assumed that young children were best cared for at home because where they would receive the one-on-one care required at this age level.

For a variety of social and economic reasons, we have largely given up the belief that young children are not ready to learn

the three R's. Today it is widely assumed that unless preschoolers are introduced to beginning reading, writing, and arithmetic, they will not be adequately prepared to enter first grade. Yet
this change in our views regarding the efficacy of early childhood education is not based on evidence of benefits of giving
academic training to young children. In fact, the preponderance of research suggests the opposite.

Our changed attitude toward the educability of young children does reflect changed attitudes regarding what is socially
acceptable family life. Among these is the contemporary acceptance of divorce, of mothers working, and of single parenting.

As these new changes in the family have become the accepted norm, they have created problems for the care of young
children. Two-parent and single-parent working families can
no longer afford someone staying at home to rear young children. As a result, there has been an extraordinary expansion
of public and private programs for young children. When I
was president of the National Association for the Education of
Young Children in the late 1980s we had only thirty thousand
members. Today there are over a hundred thousand members.

These considerations make it clear why the arguments for
the academic preschool are not factually based. Preschool is
important particularly for those children not growing up in an
experientially rich and manipulatively inviting environment.
Administrators trying to get money for full-day kindergartens
to meet the demands of working parents use the idea of educational benefits of these programs to support their arguments.

Also, it must be confessed, some parents feel less guilty about
leaving young children in early education programs rather than
in traditional play-oriented programs. These parents fall prey to
the belief that education is a race and that the earlier you start

the better. But education is not a race, and we stop learning only when we stop living.

The truth is that young children are learning a tremendous amount, but of the kind and in the manner that is appropriate for them—namely, through play. Imposing the elementary curriculum at the preschool level is as inappropriate as imposing the junior high school curriculum on elementary school students, or the high school curriculum on junior high school students.

The curricula at these higher grades are generally adapted to these age groups level of maturing intellectual abilities and interests. And that is what the traditional play preschool does as well. Both educational research and educational practice give solid evidence that young children do better with a play preschool curriculum than with an academic one. If you as a parent have a choice, let the research be your guide.

Emergencies, Preparing Children For

I was surprised and very impressed with my three-year-old granddaughter Maya, who has Down syndrome, when we were eating at a restaurant. I had these reactions because when the waitress asked her name, Maya clearly said both her name and her address. Maya's response also made me think of how important it is for young children to learn basic information about themselves that they can convey in emergencies. I was reminded of a story that recently made national headlines. Two-year-old Alana Miller had picked up the phone and dialed 911 and given the operator her name and address. Her mother, who suffered from severe migraine headaches, had taught her to dial 911 when her mother had an "owie." Alana called 911 when her mother had a severe "owie" and passed out.

While this is clearly an exceptional event, I do believe children as young as three and four should be taught their name and address as a basic safety precaution. While it is true that three- and four-year-old children can also be taught to dial 911, parents have to be discriminating if they do this. In Alana's case, her mother suffered from a condition for which it might well be necessary for her daughter to call 911. Fortunately, most parents are not in that situation. But, if there is the very real likelihood that your child might need to call 911, then makes sense to prepare the child to do so. The child should be told in simple language when to make the call and how to explain what has happened to the operator.

Young children should also be taught basic first aid when they receive a cut or bruise. Attending to the injury provides the opportunity to explain how important it is to clean the area and to apply antiseptic ointment to kill the germs before putting on the bandage. It is also important to have a first-aid kit and to show children what is in it and how to use each item in the kit. The kit should be in a place that the child can easily reach. It is also important to have essential phone numbers—such as parents' workplaces, friends, and relatives—to call in an emergency easily visible, such as in large characters on the refrigerator. Children should be told that these are numbers which are to be called if there is a problem.

Empathy in Children

Empathy is a social disposition; it is our readiness to feel the pain or distress of others. There are, of course, levels of empathy. Preschool children, for example, can be sympathetic to another child when that child's pain or distress is clearly visible. Even a two- or three-year-old may attempt to comfort a peer who is crying or clearly in pain. What young children cannot do is empathize with someone whose distress is inner rather than outer. Young children are also unaware of the hurt feelings they arouse when they loudly announce (within earshot of the individual in question), "That man's ears are so big, Mommy." Children learn not to make that kind of public comment only at the age of six or seven, when they can exercise more mature cognitive and emotional control.

Recent research (reported in the "Brain, The Moral" entry) suggests that the capacity for empathy is hard-wired in the adult brain. Janet Decety and her colleagues have found that empathy is also hard-wired in the brains of children. In their study, described in "Who Caused the Pain? An MRI Investigation of Empathy and Intentionality in Children," these investigators did MRIs of the brains of seventeen seven- to twelve-year-old children while they watched two videos of children under stress. In one video, the subject's obvious pain was caused by an accident. In the other video, the subject's pain was visibly inflicted by another person

In both cases the parts of the adult brain that have already been found to be activated by seeing others in distress were also activated in the brains of the children. In addition, when the pain was inflicted by another person, other parts of the brain also became active. These parts of the brain are the ones involved in thinking and reasoning, as opposed to those merely associated with feelings and emotions. Apparently, when one person inflicts pain on another, it goes beyond emotional resonance and brings the cognitive issues of morality and justice into play.

Although the response to others' distress may be hard-wired, how we respond to that distress depends on other factors. Children learn by imitation, and how children react to their empathic responses to the distress of another will depend, in part, at least, on what they have learned from their parents. If we are sympathetic to, rather than annoyed by, a child who is cranky, upset, or frightened, the child will internalize that empathic response. Likewise, when a child says something hurtful to another, like the remark about a person's big ears, asking him or her to say they are sorry is not helpful because the child does not understand what he or she is apologizing for. Taking the child aside and telling him or her that the remark made the other person feel bad will help the child to appreciate that words can be hurtful.

Research shows that children have a natural disposition to be sympathetic to others in distress. The extent to which that disposition is realized, however, depends vary much upon social learning.

F

Family Day Care

Of the many child care options for infants and young children, family day care has much to recommend it. Family day care is essentially an arrangement whereby the child is cared for in the home of another unrelated family. The most common family day care providers are women who are rearing, or who have reared, their own children and are experienced at child care. The family day care arrangement has several potential advantages in comparison to the day care center.

1. In the family day care arrangement, particularly in those settings where only a few children are cared for, your infant or toddler will receive the appropriate one-on-one care when it is needed.
2. In many communities you can find a family day care setting close to your home. Having a place where it is easy to drop off and pick up your child is a plus for busy parents.

3. Family day care providers are likely to be more flexible with drop-off and pickup hours. This is particularly important if a parent's job requires long or unusual hours.

4. Another advantage is that your child will have a consistent caregiver during the early years. This may not be as true for day care centers, where staff turnover is often fairly rapid.

5. If the family day care arrangement works out well for you, you may even put more than one of your children in this setting. Family day care providers, who are associated with your family long-term, almost become members of your family.

6. Last but not least, the cost of family day care is likely to be the same, or even less, than the fees at a day care center.

In choosing a family day care arrangement, you can contact one of the many online services that list the providers in your area. Alternatively, you can ask friends and neighbors with young children whom they use, or how they found the person who cares for their children. Once you have located a few providers, you should make sure that each has been licensed by the local, state, or provincial government. Licensing ensures that the setting meets minimum standards with regard to safety, cleanliness, toileting facilities, and number of children cared for.

Ideally, a single caregiver should have no more than two or three infants and toddlers; six is the maximum. In addition, you need to request references from at least three other families that have used the provider. You also need to sit down together in advance to discuss fees, hours, routines, and emergencies, leaving as little to chance as possible.

Most important when you visit the home is letting your parental radar guide you with respect to the provider and the setting. Do you really feel confidant and at ease leaving your child with this person in this setting? If not, continue your search. A feeling of security and peace of mind are really worth the time and trouble it takes to find a provider with whom you can leave your children.

Fantasy, The Uses Of

Around Easter time each year I am reminded of the question I am often asked about whether we should tell young children about the Easter Bunny, the tooth fairy, Santa Claus, and fairy tales in general. What parents fear is that when their children get older and discover that these stories are not true, they will think that their parents have lied to them. While such parental concern is entirely understandable, it comes from an adult perspective, not a child's perspective. To appreciate the child's perspective, we have to recall a little bit about child development.

Young children think differently than we do. It is not a wrong way of thinking, just different and age-appropriate. As they mature, children will overcome their earlier modes of thought themselves. The world of the young child is magical rather than scientific. In this magical world, animals can talk and think, Santa can fly through the sky in a reindeer-driven sleigh, and the tooth fairy can fly into our bedrooms, take a tooth from under an occupied pillow, and leave a gift in its place. In the same way, children believe in the characters of fairy tales, and more recently in the characters of television, such as Elmo, Miss Piggy, and Barney.

So the Easter Bunny, Santa Claus, and fairy tale characters are entirely in keeping with the young child's magical thinking. Supporting young children's belief in Santa Claus, the Easter Bunny, the tooth fairy, and fantasy actually contributes to a child's healthy development. By allowing and encouraging these fantasies with our children, we give them the feeling that we adults are able to share their perspective. In so doing, we are able to bond more closely with them.

Moreover, what parents need to appreciate is that as children mature they use their earlier beliefs in the Easter Bunny, etc., as markers of their growing maturity. I recall visiting and elementary school at Easter time and seeing a second grader pinning up paper cutouts of the Easter Bunny and baskets of colored eggs. He noticed me watching him and said to me quite proudly, "I don't believe in the Easter Bunny any longer." So children do not really resent us for having told them about fantasy characters. Actually, the reverse is more likely to be true. Our children will be thankful that we allowed them to enjoy the magical world they could later give up as a signpost of their progress toward adulthood.

Fears and Rituals

I recall that as a child I saw a movie in which a dead body fell out of a closet. For a long time after that I made sure that there was nothing in my closet before I went to bed. Even so, I would still wake up frightened of what might come out of that closet. Such fears are common in childhood, and they have many causes, but seeing something scary at a movie or on TV is a frequent starting point for such anxieties.

Fears and night terrors are usually not long-lived. Other fears may be learned and can be lasting. One young girl I saw, when I was a practicing psychologist, had acquired a fear of live chickens from her mother, who was deathly afraid of them. Another child who came to my office had developed a fear of books, which was a displaced fear of a hated aunt who insisted on reading to her. Fears of this sort, of chickens or of books, are true phobias—fears with a traumatic cause. Such long-lived fears require treatment to alleviate them.

Ritualistic behavior in young children is also very common. It is their way of controlling their world, which is in many ways ruled by adults. In young children, from two to four years of age, rituals may involve rigid routines centered on eating, bathing, and bedtime. Among three- to five-year-old children, rituals are a bit more elaborate and may appear as repeated themes in their solitary play. Such themes are sometimes seen in repetitive counting or repeatedly knocking over something they have built. Such rituals are often used by children as means of dealing with resentment, fears, and anxieties.

While a certain amount of ritualistic behavior is a normal and healthy means of dealing with stress and anxiety, if carried to extremes it can be symptomatic of a more serious problem. One young boy I saw was so insistent that his toy trucks and cars be in the same place and facing the same way that he would go into a panic if they were displaced in any way. A panic reaction to a break in the ritual or the placement of things is perhaps the best clue to what is labeled obsessive-compulsive disorder (OCD). While some obsessive-compulsive behavior is no more than a temperamental disposition toward order and detail, it becomes OCD when the individual becomes so anxious that he or she cannot function without the order and routine.

In children, and adults as well, OCD is often a way of dealing with guilt over a past action or inaction, in which case it is a way of avoiding punishment. In other cases, OCD is used as a way of controlling impulses that would be socially unacceptable if openly expressed. If you suspect that your child has OCD, it is best to get a professional opinion from your pediatrician or a child psychologist or psychiatrist. OCD is very treatable, and the earlier it is detected and dealt with the more successful the outcome.

Feelings

Young children develop the ability to feel and express the basic emotions of pain, pleasure, fear, and anger very early. In very young children, these are often expressed in extreme ways, such as anger tantrums. From an early age, however, we can begin to help young children to label and manage their feelings and emotions. Even with infants, we can say things like, "I can tell, you really like your warm bath." Or, "I guess you really don't like squash, I can tell by your unhappy face." Although the infant and young child may not understand your words, they are comforting, and more importantly, they get you into the habit of reading your child's emotional expressions and responding to them.

This tuning in to your child's feelings pays big dividends as he or she grows older. The process of tuning actually prepares you for the next important step in helping your child develop healthy emotional coping skills. This next step is accepting the child's emotions even when you think they are uncalled for. Feelings are not logical, and you cannot argue a child out of them. What is really meaningful for the child is helping him or her to understand that the emotions expressed are okay, normal, and healthy. As your child grows older you can help your child by giving him or her labels for their feelings. Giving children labels for their feelings helps them acknowledge them and bring them under control.

You can also help your child find acceptable ways to express his or her feelings. "Yes, you have every right to be angry. It was wrong for Bobby to take that toy away from you. You should tell him how mad that makes you and that he should not do it again." We can also give children words to describe, and not just label, their emotions. "Looks like you are as happy as a dog with a juicy bone."

You can also provide a physical way of describing and handing strong feelings. Sometimes when a child is really angry we can give him or her a pillow to punch to get the feelings out in a physical way.

It is also important to set limits to emotional expression. "Look, you can tell me how angry you are at me, but you cannot hit or kick me." Saying these things does not always stop an attack, which you have to stop in a physical way. But if you help your child to label feeling and give him or her acceptable outlets for them, the child will find limits easier to accept. What children need to learn is that negative feelings and emotions are healthy and normal as long as they are expressed in words and not in actions.

Flu, The

Influenza, the flu, is more serious than the common cold in children. While it is almost impossible to prevent children from catching the common cold, it is possible to lower the risk of their contracting the flu. Although some parents regard the flu as a stomach bug, flu symptoms are more severe and long lasting.

The flu is caused by one of three types of viruses. Types A and B are the familiar yearly viruses, while Type C brings about sporadic, mild symptoms. Flu is highly contagious and spreads when people are in close quarters as in a store, in a theater, on a plane, or in school classrooms. You catch the flu if you inhale air carrying infected droplets coughed or sneezed by the infected person. A person can be contagious a day before symptoms appear and for a five- to seven-day period after the symptoms are gone.

When a child catches the flu, the symptoms appear right away and are the worst over the first few days. The symptoms may include:

- A high-grade fever up to 104 degrees
- Chills and shakes with the fever
- Extreme tiredness
- Headaches and body aches
- Dry, hacking cough
- Sore throat
- Vomiting and belly pain

If your child contracts the flu, make sure to watch for complications, particularly for children under the age of two. Complications can include a sinus infection, an ear infection, or pneumonia. You should call your doctor if the fever lasts for more than a few days, or if your child complains of difficulty breathing, is congested in the face and head, or seems to be getting worse.

Flu symptoms can be treated with many over-the-counter medications. But antibiotics, while useful in treating bacterial infections, are of no use against the flu virus.

In addition to getting plenty of rest and drinking lots of fluids, children can be given over-the-counter child-size formulations of pain relievers such ibuprofen and acetaminophen.

The FDA recommends that children four years of age and younger *not* be given over-the-counter cough and cold medications (syrups and the like). Consult your pediatrician before giving your child any over-the-counter cold or flu medicine other than ibuprofen and acetaminophen. And make sure your child gets plenty of bed rest and consumes a lot of liquids.

The best way to ensure that your child is protected against the flu is to have him or her vaccinated every year. Some children six months to eight years of age may need two doses of the flu vaccine. This is particularly true for children who are being vaccinated for the first time. Your health care professional can advise you as to whether your child requires one dose or two.

Flu shots cannot guarantee that your child will not get the flu, but they do significantly reduce the risk of that occurring. Helping your child to acquire the habit of washing his or her hands before meals and after playing with friends is another important preventive measure.

Food Strikes

One of the challenging issues for parents is the need to continually alter child rearing strategies as the child matures. For example, during the first months of life the rule is to gratify all of the infants needs to the extent that this is possible. The infant is relatively helpless and completely dependent. But by the end of the first year the infant has developed a certain amount of independence and skills. At this point, parents need to distinguish between needs and wants.

Needs are those demands that are necessary for the child's healthy development. Wants, on the other hand, are things that may be pleasing to the infant but which may not be healthy. To illustrate, a one-year-old may develop a taste for sweets or starches, but too much of either is not healthy. The child may want them but certainly not need them.

The baby's increasing drive toward activity and independence may also clash with parents' interests and concerns. One example is at the end of the first year, when the baby wants to feed himself or herself. When allowed to do this, the baby gets food on the floor, walls, and all over himself or herself. As parents we decide (understandably) that the baby is not ready for self-feeding and once again take over this activity. As we did when the baby was younger, we feed him or her with a spoon, and hold the cup up for him or her to drink from.

When we do this, what often happens is that the baby goes on a food strike, cries and complains, knocks the spoon or cup out of our hands, and is generally a pain. At this point, if we are wise, we will appreciate that the baby needs (not wants) to engage in self-feeding and that it is best to allow him or her to do so. The mess can be minimized if we put less milk in the cup and less food in the bowl, and replenish these as needed. The baby will go back to enjoying his or her meal and will develop better skills and coordination. It will not take long before decorating the kitchen with food gives way to effective and relatively neat eating behavior.

As parents we many sometimes have to put up with a little mess to accommodate the child's healthy needs for activity and skill development. If we take the mess in stride and appreciate that it will be short-lived, the stress can be averted and the child will be supported in his or her increasing independence and skill development.

G

Gender Differences

Gender differences are a reality, but their origin is unclear. Some gender differences do seem to be, in part at least, genetically linked. Girls, on the average, talk earlier than boys and are more verbal in general. Boys are more likely than girls to engage in aggressive play. While girls seem to socialize on the basis of personality and appearance, boys tend to socialize around activities, mainly sports. Although boys and girls are comparable in overall intelligence, boys on average do better on tests of spatial ability and girls on tests of verbal facility. It must be remembered that these are not absolute but overlapping differences so that some boys may have exceptional verbal skills and some girls have really extraordinary spatial abilities.

Other sex differences seem to be primarily acquired rather than innate. Differences in mathematical and scientific aptitude appear, in part at least, attributable to traditional child rearing practices. Despite the efforts of the women's movement, gender differences are socially marked at birth. Often, girls are dressed in pink, boys in blue; girls are given dolls, while boys are given blocks and Legos. One consequence is that boys have more experience with combining and taking apart units than do girls. This early unit experience may well account for why boys, on the average, do better than girls on math tests. Doll play may well enhance girls' social and caring skills, while these are less developed in boys. Strong innate ability and non conventional parenting practices helps explain why some women are extraordinary mathematicians and some men are superb nurses. Again, while there are overall differences, they are overlapping and far from absolute.

Last are those gender differences that are thrust upon us. First and foremost among these is the socially constructed, and historically recent, cult of thinness for women. Particularly today, with the power of the mass media in the US, the ideal of female thinness is as virulent in small towns as it is in big cities. Some 80 percent of college women are on one or another diet, least often prescribed by a doctor and most often taken from a book or a magazine article. Similar, although it has abated a bit, is the cult of the macho male. Our movies and TV series are still dominated by the stereotype of the strong male hero à la James Bond. Gender differences are important, but they should not blind us to the character traits of kindness, fairness, and generosity, which are not sex linked, and which are the ones that make us truly human.

Gender Identity

At our children's school at Tufts, we once enrolled a boy who insisted he wanted to be a girl, who befriended girls, played

with girl toys, and sometimes put on dresses. Although all children may express some cross-sex preference at one time or
another, this is usually more a matter of passing curiosity than
of a real predilection.

But for some boys, like the one we enrolled in our school,
it was more than a passing interest. This boy (such cross-sex
preferences are usually more observable in boys than in girls)
said that he was really a member of the opposite sex, showed a
preference for cross-gender roles in fantasy play, and a preference for playmates of the opposite sex.

Such children pose a real challenge for both parents and
teachers. The parents of the boy in our school, like most parents
of children who show cross sex-preferences, were upset, confused, and felt guilty. His father was particularly angry, feeling
perhaps that his son's behavior reflected on his own masculin-
ity. The parents' attempts to get the boy to behave as a boy made
him increasingly angry and sad.

At school, although the teachers were accepting, the other
children began to regard him as odd and to tease him. With
helpful modeling by the teachers, the children came to accept
his unusual behavior. We anticipated that this boy would encounter real difficulty when he entered public school.

Longitudinal research studies of children with cross-sex
preferences suggest that although some children appear, at
least in part, to be genetically programmed for a homosexual
orientation, others are not. There are generally two approaches
to children who show consistent cross-sex preferences.

One is to see it as a normal variation of sexual identity
rooted in a particular combination of genes and hormones.
This approach leads to acceptance of the child's orientation and

to helping him or her to cope with societal norms as best the child can. Such adaptation will lessen but not eliminate some of the rejection and teasing.

The other approach is to regard such preferences as something that is learned and that can be unlearned. Parents who adopt this approach make vigorous attempts to get the boy or girl into age-appropriate activities and may even send the child to therapy.

Although psychiatry previously labeled such children as having a gender identity disorder, the current *Diagnostic and Statistical Manual of Mental Disorders* (often simply called "the DSM") now labels those with a homosexual orientation as having sexual dysphoria, but only if they are unhappy with this orientation. I believe the current label is as misguided as the last. Indeed, it is in direct contradiction to psychiatry's removal, several decades ago, of homosexuality from its list of disorders. Labeling this cross-sex preference as a dysphoria suggests that it is learned and that it can be changed. Yet homosexuality is universal and has been with us since the beginning of recorded history. It is also present in animals.

A child does not wish to be born with a cross-sex preference. Indeed may, initially at least, consider it a curse. And it is certainly not the fault of parents. For schools, the challenge is to intercept teasing and bullying by modeling accepting behavior. For parents, the real challenge is to mourn for the child they had hoped to have and to accept, love, and support the child that they were given.

It appears that our society is increasingly accepting of homosexuality, and hopefully this will make the school experiences of gay young people less traumatic.

Gifted and Talented Children

When I listen to some of the things my preschool-age grand-children come up with, such as statements like, "Are you really serious?" I am tempted to think that they are intellectually gifted and may require advanced education. But young children's language is often far in advance of their understanding, and is really not a good index of their mental powers. Albert Einstein, for example, did not speak until he was four.

Exceptionally bright children (with IQs of 140 or more) show their intellectual prowess early and in many different ways; they usually talk and read earlier than most children (Einstein was an exception) and have comprehension way beyond their years. Intellectually gifted children are always avidly in search of new information and new experiences. Parents of such children do not have to worry about providing intellectual stimulation for them; they will always find it on their own. The real task for parents of very bright children is to make sure they spend enough time developing their social and emotional skills in addition to their intellectual gifts.

It is also important to distinguish between intellectual giftedness—measured by the IQ—and talent, which is measured by precocity in a special domain, such as mathematics, music, or painting. Intellectual giftedness and talent are not highly correlated. Our most talented people are usually not intellectually gifted. Many famous writers, painters, and musicians would probably not be admitted to Mensa, the organization for those with IQs over 150. Similarly, highly intellectually gifted people may not always be successful in life. For both the intellectually gifted and the talented, the realization of their inborn abilities requires motivation as well as sheer ability. Many gifted or talented individuals never realize their potential because of personality limitations.

How parents deal with intellectual giftedness depends upon the child's level of intellectual ability. For children with IQs considerably above average, like 130 to 140, the best solution is to promote the child one year in school. This provides the intellectual stimulation the child needs and does not remove the child too far from his or her age group. In addition, it has the advantage of not stigmatizing the child by placing him or her in "gifted classes."

Unfortunately, some parents insist on putting their children in gifted classes even when this is really not warranted. An unhappy result can be that the child "fails giftedness."

A better terminology is "advanced placement" courses, which avoids the whole issue of giftedness.

For children with very high IQs—above 160—special schools for gifted children are the best answer. These children are so far beyond their age-mates that they may be treated as weird. I recall one gifted second grader who, when asked to write about the color he liked, wrote about Picasso's Blue Period. He was laughed at. Such children really need to go to a school with children at their own level.

For parents of very talented children, clear guidelines have been provided by Benjamin Bloom in *Developing Talent in Young People*. This investigator and his colleagues studied forty young people who had attained eminence by the age of forty. The life histories of these individuals were consistent in showing that in every case the parents supported and encouraged the child's own inclinations. These parents facilitated their children's spontaneous interests by providing appropriate materials and positive support, but without too much guidance or intervention. Every subject in the study expressed deep appreciation for this type of parenting.

We can't create intellectual giftedness or talents, but once they reveal themselves, we need to do everything in our power to support and facilitate—but not to push—the child to fully realize his or her potential.

Grandparents

As a grandparent first and a child psychologist second, I have learned to exercise a lot of self-discipline. Please understand that my wife and I are fortunate in having three thoughtful, considerate sons and their loving and caring wives. They have given us four grandchildren (who are, of course, extraordinary). Well aware of my feelings about hurrying and over-programming children, my sons and daughters-in-law do their best to resist the parental and societal pressures to push their children to grow up fast.

Likewise, my wife and I do our best to reinforce their opposition to popular trends. We don't buy our grandchildren many toys, and those we do buy leave plenty of room for creativity and imagination. For example, we have purchased large rocking horses and sandboxes for each of our grandchildren. In general, we try to be supportive without being intrusive.

It is also true that we cannot control, nor can we advise, our grandchildren's other grandparents. They are extremely well intentioned, but get caught up in inflated advertising and buy too many contemporary toys and gadgets for the children. These different approaches raise the issue of the grandparent's role. Because we live longer today, many more children than ever before will know their grandparents, and over longer time periods.

For parents of young children, this can be anything from a blessing to a curse. Some grandparents are very involved with their grandchildren and serve as babysitters and all-around temps when they are needed. At the other extreme are those grandparents who feel that they have raised their children and that this is their time to relax and enjoy life. They may send cards and gifts, but otherwise stay uninvolved. Still other grandparents—and this is most often true for widowed or divorced grandparents—become intrusive and over-involved in their children's and grandchildren's lives, often without really being aware of it. And increasingly, some aging and ailing grandparents may put their children in the position of having to care for them in addition to rearing their own children.

So there are probably as many grandparent stories as there are grandparents. In the best of cases, grandparents provide children with the unconditional love that may be difficult for parents who must, of necessity, be more demanding of achievement. But it is also true that some grandparents put more pressure on the grandchildren than do the parents.

With grandparents, as with so much else in life, mothers and fathers have to take the bitter with the better. My wife and I know our children appreciate our non-intrusive approach, but they probably also worry that I am constantly evaluating their child rearing. They also appreciate the loving, and well-meaning but over-done, gift giving of the other grandparents. Children are the ones who benefit the most from grandparents. That is why most parents should consider grandparents a plus, even when they are not all the parents might have wished, either for themselves or for their own children.

H

Halloween Fun and Safety

It is always a bit of a surprise to see a tall ghost when we open our door on Halloween. Some young adolescents find it hard to give up the practice of trick-or-treating. And many people, particularly young adults, use the holiday as an excuse to have elaborate dress-up costume parties. The attraction of Halloween for both children and adults is the opportunity to take on a different identity in a socially acceptable venue. We all want, and indeed need, to get out of ourselves at times, and this is particularly true for children. Children are relatively small and powerless, and dressing up in a costume gives them the chance to imagine themselves as someone they might like to be (the current music idol) or something they might otherwise fear (a ghost, a witch).

While Halloween is fun for both children and adults, it does not come without its risks. More child accidents happen on Halloween than on any other holiday. The American Academy of Pediatrics offers a number of helpful, commonsense tips on making Halloween safe for everyone involved. For parents, it is important to ensure that the front porch is well lighted and that the steps are clear of wet slippery leaves so common at this time of year. As for treats, the best course is commercially wrapped candy rather than anything homemade. Although well-intentioned, children do not appreciate toothbrushes and toothpaste as a treat. (My sons stopped going to the dentist who always handed these out in lieu of candy.)

As for children, costumes that are well fitted and that are made of fire-resistant fabric are the best. Hypoallergenic make-up is preferable to masks, which may limit the child's vision. Most children prefer make-up to masks, so it is usually not a problem. If the costume involves props like swords or pitchforks, make sure these are soft, smooth, and pliable. It is also a good practice to put strips of reflective tape on the back and sleeves of the child's costume. If children go out after dark, they should have a strong flashlight with fresh batteries.

There are other common-sense cautions that should be remembered. Children under the age of six or seven should never go out on their own; they should go out only with parents or older children. Whether young or older, children should always go out in groups and never go out alone. Before going out, children should be cautioned never to go into a person's car or house, and to go only to those houses which are well lighted and welcoming. Finally, serving children a good, even scary, Halloween dinner may keep tummies full until the children get home and the loot can be inspected and sorted out.

Halloween can be, and should be, an enjoyable, fun time for children and adults alike. Taking a few precautions can ensure that it is just that.

Handedness

The other night we went to hear a performance by a local group of musicians. It was a three-piece band with one man and two women. They all played the guitar and sang with beautiful voices. What struck me when I was watching them was that the two women held their guitars in the opposite direction from the way in which the man held his. I realized that he was left-handed and that was why he was playing the strings with his left hand and not his right. He appeared to use the same guitars as the two women so he must have adapted his playing to the standard guitar. Perhaps I was particularly attuned to this because I noticed, while watching President Obama on TV, that he was signing legislation with his left hand.

Handedness in infants appears fairly early. Even during the first few months, you may notice that your baby holds one hand more fisted than another, waves one hand more vigorously, or lies with their head turned more toward one side or the other. Those who study infants report that about 60 to 70 percent of infants are likely to turn their heads more to the right than to the left. In many cases (certainly not all), this can be a sign of later handedness. By four to six months the signs are a bit clearer. At this age, most infants will hold a rattle or spoon longer in one hand than in the other. You can also tell hand preference at this age by noticing which hand the infant uses to reach for an object whether it is on their right or left sides. But infants are ambidextrous and continue to use the non-preferred hand a lot of the time.

By the end of the first year, the infant's motor control is pretty advanced, and about 70 percent of this age group will hold a toy with moving parts with the left hand and manipulate the parts with the right. About one in seven children manipulate the moving part with their left hand, and a like number don't seem to have a preference. By two years of age a child's hand preference is pretty pronounced. The preferred hand is now used in most everyday activities, and the number of children at this age who show no clear preference goes down. By the age of three and four, with the development of fine motor control, children show a clear hand preference in their drawing and writing.

Not too long ago, left-handedness was regarded as a handicap, and some children showing left-handedness were forced to use their right. Not surprisingly, this produced a variety of emotional problems. Handedness is brain determined, and is a pretty fixed trait. In today's high-tech world, left-handedness is much less an issue than it was in the past. And it does not seem to hinder those with high intelligence or athletic or artistic talent. So if your child is a lefty, just be thoughtful when buying gifts or sports or music equipment and choose things that are suited for him or her.

Happiness, What Children Will Need Most For

In 2009 *The Atlantic* published a riveting article by Joshua Wolf Shenk called "What Makes Us Happy?" reviewing a study that followed 268 Harvard graduates over the last seventy-two years. The original aim of the study was to determine which factors were essential to a full and successful life. The study began in the late 1930s and followed these men through their war service, marriages, careers, parent- and grandparenthood, and old age, or until their death. Initially they were given a wide battery of tests, questionnaires, and interviews. The funding for the study eventually gave out. But in the late 1960s, the study was revived by psychiatrist George Vaillant, who has been in charge of the investigation ever since. Vaillant has continued to personally conduct interviews with the surviving participants.

While many of the participants did well, including President Kennedy, others did not. But the major finding of the study is that the life course of an individual is almost impossible to predict. Human beings are extraordinarily complex, as is the world we live in. Nonetheless, two things stood out in the lives of those participants who had the most productive and the happiest lives, underscoring what we have known to be true for a long time. Regardless of life circumstance, those who did best had someone who loved them deeply and made them feel that they were important in that person's life. A similar message comes from the life histories of those who have risen from poverty such, Oprah and Dolly Parton.

Another finding about what children need most comes from a parallel longitudinal study, undertaken at about the same time, to determine the causes of delinquency. A group of delinquents was paired with a comparable group of non-delinquent boys from working class, largely immigrant families. Vaillant took over this study and has been following as many of the participants as he and his colleagues could find.

As opposed to the low-income young men who had become delinquent, those who had not had one significant difference in their life histories. The men who became successful in their occupations had worked or had engaged in organized team sports when they were teenagers. These activities apparently taught these young men a work and responsibility ethic, which they carried forward into adult life.

These two findings seem to support what Freud said in answer to the question of what was most necessary to live a full and happy life. He replied, "Lieben und arbeiten," loving and working. But as I read some of the interviews, it seemed to me that a third factor was also involved. Those who succeeded did not take themselves too seriously and had a sense of humor. So I believe that we need to add "spielen"—play—to love and work as the necessary components to a full, productive, and happy life.

Head Bumps

Each winter, when our three sons were young, we took them to the Caribbean for a couple of weeks to escape the harsh Rochester, New York, snow and cold. One year we went to Curacao. After we got to our hotel room and were getting unpacked, our middle son, a five-year-old, began jumping up and down on the bed to discharge some of the energy he had accumulated over a long plane ride.

Before I could stop him, he fell back and hit his head on the metal bed frame. He did not lose consciousness, but blood gushed from a large cut on the back of his head. We stopped most of the bleeding, called the emergency room at the hospital, and I broke the speed limit to get him there. But we were outside the town, which can only be entered by crossing a drawbridge. The bridge was up, and we had to wait to cross. When we finally got to the hospital, the doctor put in about six stiches and we returned home.

Head injuries are more common in young children than in any other age group. Their heads are larger in proportion to the rest of their bodies, relative to older children and adults, so they are top-heavy. They also have less muscle strength and motor control, so falls and bumps are almost the rule. And like my son, they are also always testing the limits.

Most such accidents happen quickly—a slip in the tub, a fall when attempting to climb stairs, a bump against furniture or other children. Most head injuries in children are not serious, because the skull provides protection and because the brain is most resilient at this time of life. They can usually be treated with first aid: washing and applying an antiseptic and a Band-Aid. For more serious injuries, like my son's, emergency room treatment and stiches may be in order.

For most such head bumps, there are some simple rules to follow. First, stay calm. Then, follow these rules:

- If there is an open cut, clean it and apply pressure to stop the bleeding. If the cut is longer than about an inch or is near the eyebrow, you should take your child to the emergency room or to your pediatrician.
- If the cut is a small one, taping the edges of the cut together after applying an antiseptic can help the healing of a superficial wound.
- Make sure your child rests but does not sleep for at least two hours. Keep a close watch on his or her behavior.
- Don't give your child pain relievers. Give him or her only clear liquids during this time.

If you suspect that your child may have had a more serious injury, watch him or over the next twenty-four hours for any symptoms of a concussion. For babies:

- Bulges at the fontanels (the soft spots where the skull has not yet hardened)

- Vomiting
- Lethargy
- High-pitched crying

For children older than one:

- Vomiting or nausea
- Sensitivity to light and noise
- Headaches
- Sluggishness or grogginess
- Pupils that are bigger than normal or of unequal size
- Problems with concentration and memory
- Confusion

It is very important to write down any observed symptoms before you take your child to see the doctor. The symptoms are very helpful in making a diagnosis. Fortunately, as mentioned earlier, the young brain is very resilient, and most head bumps, even those involving concussions, have no lasting detrimental consequences.

High-Energy Children

In the 1920s and 1930s, pediatrician Arnold Gesell and his colleagues Frances L. Ilg and Louise Bates Ames photographed, observed, and interviewed hundreds of children from one to sixteen years of age. They published several books, such as *The Child from Five to Ten* and *The First Five Years of Life*, that gave profiles for each year level. These profiles have stood the test of time and are still quite applicable to today's children.

During a trip to Hawaii, I was reminded of Gesell's description of six-year-olds as being in constant motion—running, talking, climbing, eating non-stop. Our granddaughter just turned six, and she behaves as if she were one of Gesell's subjects. She directed us to her school and spent most of the time there on the climbing apparatus and even made use of the ones for the older children (it was school vacation and there were no other children about). In the car, when there was a lull in the conversation, she would ask why no one was talking. At the beach, she challenged me to a race, which I accepted—and regretted later as the pains came on.

Heather's constant activity also reminded me of an experience I had earlier in my career, when I worked as a school psychologist for the city of Boston. I was fresh out of grad school and still quite green when it came to children—I had been trained to work with adults. In one school I was assigned to, I visited a first grade classroom. One boy caught my eye. He was running about the room, talking to his friends, watering the flowers—a general whirlwind of activity. I suggested to the teacher that he was showing signs of hyperactivity and might be suffering from "minimal brain injury," the fad diagnosis of that era. The teacher only laughed and said, "Oh no, he's just all boy." And then she introduced me to Gesell, who, along with Piaget, became one of my mentors.

I tell this story because no one seems to read Gesell anymore. Today when I visit a first grade classroom and see a boy acting in the manner of the boy I had seen years earlier, the teacher is likely to believe that he has ADHD and needs to be put on Ritalin. Child development is a very small part of contemporary teacher training, and Gesell and Piaget are now thought to be passé.

Today it is believed that teachers need to learn about culture and diversity, not about development. Culture and diversity are important, but so is development. We are biological as well as social beings. The neglect of biological growth has led to the serious narrowing of the range of normality for children and youth. One result of this narrowing is the widespread misdiagnosis and uncalled-for drug treatment of children and youth. Where are Gesell and Piaget when we need them?

Home-Schooling

One of the questions I am most frequently asked in my talks with parents has to do with my views on home-schooling. There are several reasons for these questions. Some parents are already home-schooling their children and looking for professional support for this decision. Other parents are considering the possibility and want to hear both pros and cons. Finally, some parents are opposed to it and want negative arguments to justify their position.

Based on all the research evidence I can find, and on my talks with parents and children who have participated in home-schooling, it can provide an excellent education. This is particularly true in those communities that welcome home-schooled adolescents into the local high school science labs and sports teams, which would otherwise be unavailable to them. For those parents who choose to home-school, there are now many online communities with helpful information and guidance, and many excellent curricula for purchase.

The advantages are straightforward. We know that the effectiveness of education is closely related to the amount of time the teacher has for each pupil. Home-schooling is like tutoring in this regard. In addition, home-schooled children don't have to spend part of their school day being taken to school and back home. Furthermore, parents who home-school can use the environment much more freely than can a classroom teacher. Children can visit museums, take nature walks, visit historic sites, and so on. (If we are honest, most education does not really take place in the classroom.) Last but not least, parents can individualize instruction according to the child's particular interests and abilities. A home-schooled boy in northern California taught himself to read when he was nine because he was raising goats and wanted to explore books and articles about the best way to do this. He later went on to Harvard and to a successful medical career.

It should be said, however, that home-schooling is not for everyone and is probably not the wave of the future. Most parents do not have the time, or the financial resources, to home-school. It also takes a dedication and commitment that are not commonplace. And there are the limitations of not being in a school system with science and sports facilities. But for those parents who choose to go this route, it can be an exciting challenge, and for home-schooled children, it can be a richly rewarding experience.

Homework

For many teachers, parents, and children, homework is a fighting word. Some regard homework as all positive, reinforcing good work habits, discipline, and responsibility. Others see it as all bad, as rote, meaningless, and as a major contributor to children's dislike of school and learning. Both positions ignore the fact that there is a wide variety of homework practices, some of which are very supportive of positive attainments, and some of which probably do harm. The real problem is being able to recognize which homework is worth the effort put into it.

I believe there are three criteria for judging the value of homework. The first is that it be meaningful and have real educational value. When I taught a small seminar at Tufts University, I had students do a number of papers over the course of the semester. Because there were relatively few students in the class (ten to twelve), I was able to read and comment on each of their papers. This type of homework was a learning experience for the students and for me. An example of worthless homework is an assignment that is merely checked off as being turned in and never actually read.

The second criterion is that the homework be age-appropriate. Age-appropriateness has to do with both the content and the amount of schoolwork to be done at home. For elementary school students, particularly those in the early grades, two hours of homework is the most that should be required and should be limited to math and reading assignments. Children at this age need to be active and engaged in a variety of social and extra-curricular activities.

At the secondary level, homework assignments can be in a wide range of subjects and be more complex and involved. But again, such homework is only meaningful if the teacher has the time to read and respond individually to the assignments. In public secondary schools, teachers have so many classes that only the most dedicated give each of their classes long homework assignments. It is a paradox of our school system that at the age when students can most profit from closer communication with their teachers, the distance between teachers and individual students becomes much wider.

The third criterion for assessing homework has to do the child. Some children are very conscientious and do their homework on their own without prodding or compulsion. Others resist but eventually do it with some parental pressure. Last are those who simply refuse, dawdle, or find excuses for not doing what is required, even when this is minimal. This often sets the stage for some intense parent-child conflicts. Usually, the conflicts just make matters worse.

I think it is a bad idea for parents to get too involved in a child's homework assignments. Certainly helping with a particular problem or answering a particular question does no harm, and can help cement parent-child relations. But over-involvement—overseeing the entire project—is a mistake. It is much better to get an older neighborhood child to come in and tutor the child. Usually, children will accept such a tutor if they are at least four years older—so they do not feel that a peer is tutoring them. Most young people profit from such tutoring, and it avoids an endless parent-child standoff.

Accordingly, there are some general criteria for assessing the value of homework, but these have to be tempered by taking the particular child into account. For some children it is an exciting challenge, and for others sheer drudgery. Overall, as I noted above, I see little need for homework, other than reading books and doing math for children in the first few grades. Thereafter, the amount of homework should never cut seriously into the young person's time for play and socialization. And it should always be a meaningful communication between teacher and student if it is to be a valuable and worthwhile educational experience.

Illness, Talking with Children About

Our fourteen-year-old dachshund, Remy, has been a nanny to our granddaughters and grandnieces. When they were infants, he growled when strangers came near and paid no attention when the girls pulled his ears or tail. When the girls were toddlers, they fed him under the table and tried to sleep on his bed. As they got older, a marker of maturity was being able to hold his leash when he went for his walks. At this stage, they also liked to dress him up (fortunately no make-up) and play tug-of-war with his pull toy. When they arrive at our house for a visit, he is usually the first one to get a hug.

Last summer, Remy ate something he could not pass and had to have emergency surgery. He got through that okay, after a few bouts with the medication. We told the girls that he had a tummy ache but that he was much better now. There was no need to talk about the surgery—cutting open his stomach, etc.—because that would only have frightened and upset them. They were all concerned and sent handmade get-well cards that were a real delight. Unhappily, soon after the surgery, Remy injured his back and is now prohibited from running, climbing, and jumping. For his own sake we have to keep him in a cage when we leave the house.

It is a little harder to explain this condition to young children because the illness is not visible. You have to watch him carefully to see that he favors his left hind leg. So when the girl's visit, we explain that he hurt his leg and it will get worse if we let him run, jump, or climb stairs. But other than allowing them to sit with him on the couch while watching TV, we are careful not to leave him alone with them. It is hard for young children to understand the seriousness of the problem (potential paralysis) because it is not visible. And even though we have explained the risks, children may not appreciate their seriousness and try to play with him as they always did.

Many of the same kinds of explanations and restrictions are in order when dealing with family members who are ill. Children should not be kept in the dark about illness, but it should be explained in the simplest, most concrete and least graphic ways. Again, this is easier when there is physical evidence, like a broken arm or sprained ankle.

It is more difficult when the illness is less visible, such as allergies or arthritis. For such illnesses children need to be given direct, simple explanations: "If he eats peanuts, he will get sick." "Papa's legs hurt, and that is why he walks slowly." Most children are sympathetic and understanding if they are given a simple explanation. But they should not be put in a position where, unwittingly, they might do something that might be harmful to the person with the ailment. Dementia and Alzheimer's have to be explained in the same way: "Papa tends to forget things, so he may ask you the same question, or tell you the same story. So don't be annoyed."

The problem becomes more delicate when the illness is a fatal one and a parent, grandparent, or other loved person is the one who is ill. Again, it is important to be honest with children and not to hide either the illness or its seriousness from them. Young children, before the age of five or six, do not yet grasp the concept of death and need only be told that "Papa is very sick and we have to be quiet, but we also have to tell him how much we love him." Older children can be told that "Papa will probably not get better, and we may lose him. We need to tell him how much we love him and remind him of the good times we shared together."

It is most difficult when it is the parent of young children who is dying. But the same general rules hold. We have to be honest with the children, explain in simple terms, and encourage the children not only to express their love and their sadness, but also their thanks for all that the parent has given them, and to recall the happy times they shared together. Every child is different, and in these situations the surviving parent has to adapt the information to the child's personality and the nature of the illness. But honesty, simplicity, and expressions of thanks and of loving care are always in order for those who are ill.

Infant Intelligence

Over the years a number of authors have promised parents techniques that could raise their child's IQ. To achieve this goal, parents had only to follow the program of activities described in their books. These bogus claims, which many parents take seriously, merit a piece on intelligence, particularly infant intelligence.

Let's start with a definition. The IQ (intelligence quotient), is arrived at by dividing a child's mental age by his or her chronological age. The child's MA is determined by the child's performance on a variety of tests, in comparison to the performance of the normative comparison group of same-age children (IQ 100). These tests, including those for memory, vocabulary, concept formation, and problem solving, are what define intelligence as measured by tests. A child who scores higher than the normative group will have a higher mental age than his or her chronological age, and thus a higher IQ than the norm of 100. In the same way, a child who scores lower than the normative group will have an IQ below 100.

A few additional points need to be added. First, there are no units of intelligence, and you can't perform mathematical operations upon IQs. A child with an IQ of 100 for example, is not twice as smart as a child with an IQ of 50. The IQ is simply a rank; it is no different from the points given to a competitive ice skater or gymnast. There are no units of ice skating or gymnastics either. Second, the same IQ score can indicate very different performances. For example, a child who scores high on vocabulary and low on concept formation will attain the same overall score as a child who performs at the same level on both tests. Third, the IQ is generally more determined by heredity (60–65 percent) than it is by environment (35–40 percent) except in extreme cases. Finally, the IQ generally remains constant across the life-span.

In practical terms, by the time is a child is five or six, most parents have a pretty good sense of their child's IQ (their relative brightness) and can estimate it within ten points or so. This is because in daily life, parents intuit IQ in terms of a child's language facility, readiness to learn, adaptability to new situations, and problem solving.

This brings us to the issue of infant intelligence. Most intelligence tests involve language both in the instructions given to the child and in the tests themselves. Inasmuch as infants have little or no language, it is really not possible to measure their intelligence. There are several infant intelligence scales, to be sure, but these are limited to measuring the infant's motor and attentive skills. Performance on infant intelligence scales does not predict later intellectual ability.

It should be obvious why any claims that particular activity programs increase an infant's IQ are false and misleading. There is absolutely no evidence that we can increase an infant's IQ in a programmatic way. The skills and abilities that are measured on intelligence tests can be negatively affected by extreme stimulus deprivation, but also by overzealous environmental stimulation.

By simply following and supporting babies' self-initiated activities, we can provide all the age-appropriate stimulation needed to maximize intellectual, social, and emotional development.

Infant Signing

There has been a long-standing controversy among experts in the hearing impaired field over whether learning sign language lowers a limited-hearing infant's motivation to learn to speak. Now, a similar controversy has arisen over whether or not to teach signing to hearing infants so that they can communicate before they learn to talk.

This idea came from Joseph Garcia, who, in 1999, published a book called *Sign with Your Baby: How to Communicate with*

Infants Before They Learn to Speak. Garcia was not suggesting that parents teach their children American Sign Language, the formal system of signing taught to people with limited or no hearing. Rather, he proposed that infants could be taught simple signs to communicate their wants, such as signs for "juice" or "milk."

Critics of infant signing have raised the same objections as they have to signing for the limited hearing population. Their main argument is that learning to sign will discourage the infant from learning to speak. Reports from parents who have used signing (and the number is growing rapidly in the US and abroad) are that the opposite is the case. Parents who have used signing with their infants find that their children learn to speak as early, and as well, as infants who have not learned signing.

Research studies have backed them up. A study presented in an article called "Gesture Paves the Way for Language Development," for example, found that infant signing was closely tied to their spoken language development and appeared to prepare them for it. It seems reasonable to conclude, as most in deaf education have conceded, that the most important thing is for the child to acquire the concept of communication through whatever means he or she is able.

Signing does give the infant tools to communicate specific wants, and thus limits the frustration of both infant and parent. If you decide to teach your infant to sign, here are a few simple rules to follow:

- Use the infant's spontaneous gestures (e.g., palm up) as a guide for creating signs for simple words like "more," "down," or "juice."

- Always pair the sign you are making with the word it represents.
- Be patient. Learning to sign takes time, often more than a month.
- Teach others who interact with the baby the signs that you are using.
- Make sure you praise your infant with a big smile and with words when he or she uses the sign.

A final personal note: One of my granddaughters has Down syndrome, and her parents taught her a few simple signs. She is two now, and talking up a storm. Signing certainly didn't interfere with her language development, and may well have helped it. My son and daughter-in-law did not buy any CDs or kits; they just taught Maya a few easy signs using gestures she made herself. So you really don't need to purchase anything, just keep it simple. Teaching your infant just a few signs will reduce the stress and enrich the quality of your parent-child interactions.

Instructing Young Children, Tips On

As adults, we often forget, when we are talking to children, that they think more concretely and process information at a slower pace than we do. When we adapt our instructions to children's level of understanding, we are not talking down to them. What we are doing is telling them that we understand and respect what they are saying. By doing this when our children are young, we establish the foundation for similar communication when they get to be teenagers. And that is no mean achievement.

Here are some tips for talking with young children.

1. Be specific. Instructions should be short and clear and suited to the child's level of development. One guideline is to use one word per age of the child. For example, when speaking to a two-year-old you might say, "Hat on." But to a five-year-old you might say, "Put your hat on."

2. Because children process information more slowly than we do, it's a good idea to give only one instruction at a time. A child who might be able to follow one instruction may get confused by two or more and not be able to follow any.

3. Accentuate the positive. You will have much more success, and much less frustration, if you tell children what you want them to do rather than what not to do. In addition to having a happier emotional tone, positive instructions do not give children options. If you say, "Please don't yell," you leave available the options to simply talk loudly or to mumble. If you say, "Please speak quietly," you eliminate the options. Comedian Bill Cosby learned this the hard way. When he told one of his daughters, "Young lady, I don't ever want to hear you use those words again!" she replied, "Then don't listen."

4. A very important tip is to phrase your instructions so as to *tell* the child what you want, not *ask* him or her to make the decision. Again, if you ask the child, "Do you want to put your pj's on?" you leave him or her a choice. But if you say, in a firm and pleasant voice, "Please put your pj's on," they do not have a choice.

5. It is important to thank a child who has followed an instruction. Such a response is not only good manners, it also is an appropriate reward, and has the added benefit of modeling an important social skill.

Giving meaningful, easily followed, and positive instructions has both immediate and long-term benefits for both you and your child.

Intuitions, Wrong

Recently, while in a bookstore looking for some reading material for our grandchildren, I noticed a number of books for young children dealing with everything from divorce to homosexuality and AIDS. It reminded me of how our thinking is always colored by wrong intuitions about both the physical and psychological worlds.

For example, for thousands of years we believed that the earth was flat and that if you walked to the end, you would fall off. With the advent of science we learned from the shadow of the earth on the moon and the disappearance of ships on the horizon that in fact the earth was round. In a similar way, we believed that the sun revolved around the earth until Copernicus demonstrated that the earth revolves about the sun.

We have a number of psychological intuitions that are also incorrect. This is particularly true with respect to children. Some of these intuitions are dormant until they are activated by a particular concept. The Head Start program is a case in point. The program was conceived at the height of the civil rights movement and was meant to give low-income children the kind of educational experience that would prepare them to succeed in the public schools.

Head Start is a great overall child care program, but it was never meant to raise IQs . The name "Head Start," however, elicited a dormant intuition to the effect that education is a race and that the sooner you start, the sooner and the better you finish. This false intuition has given rise to much of the academic hurrying that is so pervasive in our schools today.

Yet education is not a race, and there is no evidence that an early academic start has any lasting advantages. Indeed, all of the evidence is to the contrary. But psychological intuitions are as hard to overcome as the physical ones. Hopefully, it will not take us centuries to overcome this one.

An equally pernicious intuition about children is the idea that a bad experience is the best preparation for a good one. It is this erroneous belief that explains why I found books for young children dealing with divorce, AIDS, and child abuse. Certainly, for children who are dealing with these issues in their lives, some level of discussion may be in order. But most of the children who read, or who have these books read to them, will never need to deal with these issues until they are much older. Why put them at risk for stress, misunderstanding, and confusion for no purpose?

The truth is that a bad experience is the worst preparation for a bad experience. This was demonstrated by a recent study of children who were directly affected by the events of 9/11, that is, those who either lost a loved one or witnessed the events directly. While all of the children showed stress symptoms, only those who had a prior seriously stressful experience showed clinically significant symptoms. So, contrary to this intuition, the best preparation for a bad experience is a *good* experience. And the more good experiences children have, the better they will be prepared for whatever bad ones they will encounter later.

J

Job Loss and Family Stress

Perhaps because they are growing—constantly changing in size, in appearance, and in emotional and intellectual maturity—children thrive best in a stable environment. In a stable environment, young people can use all of the adaptive energies to coping with changes within themselves. When a parent loses his or her job, this is a major source of instability. Parents themselves change, and may become depressed and unhappy. The financial problems put stress on the marriage, and couples who got along well before may become sullen and withdrawn, or engage in frequent quarreling and recrimination.

The impact of job loss on children has been well documented. A *New York Times* article called "Job Loss Affecting Family Life" reviewed a number of such studies. A University of California, Davis, study, for example, found that children from a household in which a parent has lost a job were 15 percent more likely to repeat a grade than were children from homes where job loss had not occurred. Parents who have lost a job may be too preoccupied with their own distress to fully appreciate the impact of job on their children. Most of the research suggests that it is the changes in the emotional climate, rather than the financial sacrifices, that are the most harmful to children. Coping with parental depression and quarreling can drain the energy children need for their own personal growth and development.

Studies suggest that the impact of job loss is greater on men than it is on women. Even in our liberated society, men seem still to take the role of breadwinner as an all-important part of their identity.

When men lose their jobs they do not usually take on more household or child care responsibilities. In contrast, women who lose their jobs tend to spend more time with their children, which may help them to see at least one positive consequence of job loss. Even if parents do get new jobs, these are often at lower levels and salaries than what they had previously, and this can be a source of continued stress and unhappiness.

Some writers have argued that job loss can have benefits for the family. They argue that the family now has more time together, and spends less time on computers, the Internet, or personal hobbies like golfing. Working together to cope with financial problems can be a source of strength for children who are made to feel that they are part of the solution to the problem. While this may be true for some families, it is the exception, not the rule.

There is no simple answer to the traumas caused by job loss—during a recession or at any time. If parents appreciate that their children are hurting as much as they are, they will be open with them about the situation and involve the children in making adaptations to their new life circumstance. This can help reduce the stress for everyone.

Junk Food Addiction

We all know that junk food—edibles loaded with sugar, fat, and salt—are bad for our health. Just as plaque can build up on our teeth and gums, it can also build up on the inner walls of the veins and arteries that carry blood to and from our heart. This can predispose a person to heart attacks and other ailments. And we believe that we can dump the junk food habit, if we just set out minds to it. New research suggests that breaking the junk food habit may not be as easy as it seems.

A study published in the journal *Nature Neuroscience* titled "Dopamine D2 Receptors in Addiction-like Reward and Dysfunction and Compulsive Eating in Obese Rats" suggests that junk food can be addictive. The researchers fed a group of rats a steady diet of bacon, cheesecake, and other fat-, sugar-, and salt-laden foods. Not surprisingly, rats fed the calorie-loaded diet became obese while rats fed a healthy diet retained the normal body weight for their species.

The authors found that the junk food diet increased the release of dopamine, the "feel-good" neurotransmitter. That is, eating a consistent diet of junk food makes it harder for the brain to produce a "feel-good" response from healthy food.

This dopamine release is so powerful that the obese rats continued to stuff themselves with the rich foods even when they were administered a mild shock for doing so. Even more striking was the observation that the overweight rats starved themselves rather than eat healthy food when it was offered to them. This behavior pattern is similar to alcohol and drug addiction in humans, which is often coupled with a loss of pleasure from food and non-alcoholic liquids.

The point is that when a child eats an overabundance of any junk food, from jelly donuts to french fries, he or she can become addicted. As in the lab animals, these foods will release the dopamine that make the habituated child feel good. The fatter the child, the more difficult it is to break the habit. This is one of the reasons obese diabetics have such trouble giving up the foods they know are bad for them.

Parenthetically, one of the reasons that some children bang their heads is because banging the head tends to release dopamine. Like the rats who continue eating even when they are shocked, children continue to bang their heads despite the pain.

To be sure, a meal of junk food now and then will do no harm. It is a consistent diet of such food that does the damage. Forewarned is forewarned, and this research should help us say no when the kids want too much of the bad stuff.

K

Kindergarten, Full-Day

At a recent talk with parents I was asked about the value of full-day kindergarten. I replied that I thought that it was a child care initiative and not an educational one. I went on to explain that in this country we do not have the affordable, accessible, high-quality child care that two-parent and single-parent working families so badly need. Schools are safe, teachers are well trained, and there are ample educational materials and play areas. In the absence of quality day care, many parents prefer that their children spend a full day in kindergarten rather than half a day at school and half a day in day care. And there is no problem with full-day kindergarten so long as we remember that most five-year-olds need a nap or quiet time in the afternoon. If the kindergarten provides cots, quiet music, or teacher-read stories, the full-day kindergarten need do no harm. It is only when the afternoon is seen as additional time for academic instruction that it goes against what is in the best interests of the child.

When I was done, one woman raised her hand and, when called upon, said "I am a kindergarten teacher, I have had a full-day kindergarten, and I consider myself a teacher not a day care worker."

I responded, "To be sure the term 'day care' has a bad rep because it was initially used for those who looked after wayward or abandoned children. But in contemporary society, with over 80 percent of preschool children in one or another type of early childhood program, child care refers to the care of all young children. And it is certainly true that while teaching is a profession, much teaching is done by non-teachers. Mothers, for example, are children's first teachers.

Moreover, if we define "child care" as a concern for the child's social and emotional well being, this is certainly a concern of teachers.

Many of the best early childhood educators I know are those who are most ready to give a young child a hug when he or she needs it. And even as a college professor I am supposed to act *in loco parentis*, in the place of a parent. And I certainly try to provide comfort and support to a student who has just lost a parent or grandparent. In the end, the distinction between teacher and child care giver (in the broad sense) is a false dichotomy. Every responsible teacher is a child care giver and every good child care giver is necessarily a teacher."

Knowing vs. Understanding

I was on a radio program once with a woman who contends that she has a technique for teaching infants to read and to do math. She is but one of a large number of entrepreneurs who have started companies to produce books, videos, and training guides for parents who want to give their children an academic head start. One of the arguments offered by these promoters of early learning is that the brain grows rapidly during the first years of life and that is the time to give it the most stimulation. While it is true that the brain does reach full size by age five, it is not the size that determines how or what the child learns. Rather, it is the connection between the neurons that is critical for true understanding.

There are two basic confusions in the arguments made by those who profess to teach infants academics. One has to do with the definition of terms. Reading, for example, is a very complex skill, and we use the same term to describe many different levels of reading. Even one- and two-year-old children can, for example, learn sight words. That is, they can learn to say the name of certain words that they recognize. But this is really no different from learning to say "cat" when seeing a cat, or saying "dog" when seeing a dog. It is a form of reading to be sure, but it does not involve decoding and comprehension— what we usually mean by "reading" and which does not appear until after the age of five or six.

The same holds true for understanding numbers. Young children can learn to identify different numbers, like words, and to count. But this does not mean that the child can do addition, subtraction, and multiplication, which is what we usually mean by "math." Arithmetic operations require the mental construction of a unit. Again, this concept is only attained after reaching the age of five or six. If a child has a concept of a unit, he or she understands that the number three, for example, is like every other number in that it is in the class of numbers. But the child also understands that the number three is not like any other number in that it is the only number that comes before four and after two. It is only after the child attains the unit concept that he or she understands that a number is both ordinal and cardinal.

The second confusion is that between knowing and understanding. Knowing is on the surface, understanding is deep. Much of what is being sold to parents as reading and math instruction for infants is really teaching children to know numbers and letters. It is far removed from their ability to understand what they read or to understand *why* 2 + 2 = 4. Both of these abilities reflect understanding—an ability to mentally manipulate ideas. Knowing doesn't use much of the brain, but understanding does. Perhaps that is why Albert Einstein wrote, "Any fool can know. The point is to understand."

While the early learning programs focus on the infant's ability to know, they ignore his or her need to understand. And infants do want to understand their world, and they make every effort to do so. For example, infants bring together the different experiences of the mother's voice, smell, touch, and appearance into an organized image or whole. When this organized image is constructed, by the end of the first year, the infant appreciates that the mother exists when she is no longer present to the senses. That is a laborious and time-consuming construction, and it speaks to the young infant's need to understand, not just to know, his or her world.

The integrative efforts employed by the infant in constructing permanent objects, as well as constructing language can be undermined by the early learning programs that focus on knowing. Whereas the infant wants to learn by integration, these programs force him or her to learn by rote. The danger here is that a rote learning style will be imprinted on the infant, which will impair the use of integrative learning later.

Although a certain amount of rote is useful (say, learning the multiplication tables), it should be but one of the learning styles available to children. While there is no evidence that these early learning programs have any lasting benefits, we do have evidence that they can do lasting harm.

Parents really need to be alerted to the difference between knowing and understanding, and to value and encourage their child's need for understanding, and not just knowing, their immediate world. As Friedrich Froebel, the inventor of kindergarten so wisely said, "Children need to learn the language of things before they learn the language of words." I would add "and of numbers."

L

Learning Styles and Temperaments

The history of education is one of unending conflict between two opposing views regarding the aims of schooling. Some take the position that we grow from within—that children have their own ways of knowing and that the goal of education should be to nourish this growth. In his book *Pedagogy of the Oppressed*, famed Brazilian educator Paulo Friere called this aim "liberation." The opposing view is that of discipline from without and the belief that the goal of education should be to socialize children to be responsible citizens. Friere called this educational aim "domestication."

It is interesting that philosophers and educators who formulated and supported these opposing positions had quite different temperaments. John-Jacques Rousseau, the author of *Emile* and one of the earliest advocates for growth from within, was a free thinker in a number of domains. In addition to his educational and political tracts (which contributed to the American and French Revolutions), he wrote plays, operas, and one of the first autobiographies. In contrast, John Locke, one of the earliest advocates of discipline from without, was a compulsively orderly man who argued that all knowledge comes from experience, although he did acknowledge individual differences.

Likewise, Friedrich Froebel, the inventor of kindergarten, defied convention in both manner and dress. The curriculum materials (gifts) he created for his kindergarten charges were open-ended and encouraged creativity. One gift was a set of toothpicks and dried peas that children could use to construct different forms.

These curriculum materials were far different from those created by Maria Montessori. Although Montessori defied convention by becoming the first female physician in Italy and fighting for women's rights, she was also very disciplined and orderly. The curriculum materials she created emphasized learning the skills and concepts required for social adaptation. For example, she introduced sandpaper letters to help children learn these through touch as well as through sight.

One could argue, along with William James, that educational theory may be as much a matter of temperament as of intellectual conviction. In addition to the liberal/conservative dichotomy described above, many other such temperament dichotomies have been proposed. Darwin distinguished between scientists who were "lumpers" and those who were "splitters." Others have labeled these temperamental differences "synthetic" and "analytic," that is, some people see the forest, others the trees.

It does not seem far-fetched to argue that parents, too, vary in this type of temperament. Those who are mainly concerned with their children learning the tool skills (reading, writing, and arithmetic), getting into good schools, and so on, are likely to be on the more orderly, conventional end of the lumper-splitter temperament continuum. Those parents concerned that their children have time to play, and to be curious and imaginative, may be on the open, less conventional end.

If this interpretation is correct, perhaps we need to rethink our antipathies as to liberation and domestication. When these two orientations are thought of as intellectual preferences, we tend to see the other side as not only wrong, but also bad. But, if we were to see these orientations as reflections of human temperament, rather than wrong headedness, perhaps we would be willing to compromise and see the other side. After all, the aim of all education, as of child rearing, should be to both liberate and domesticate. In the end, the real challenge is to find ways of integrating these two orientations in a meaningful and productive fashion.

Lisping

Lisping is most often a temporary speech disorder of children who have just lost their two front teeth. Nearly 5 percent of first graders have this type of disorder. This "frontal," or "interdental," speech problem is produced when the tongue protrudes through the space between the remaining teeth. As a result, the child is unable to correctly pronounce the sounds of *s* or *z*. For example, child with this disorder will pronounce "lisp" as "lithp," substituting the *th* sound for the *s* or *z* sound.

Some children have other forms of temporary speech disorders. When our middle son was five, for example, he could not make the *l* sound and would say "yayow" for "yellow." He could clearly hear the sound correctly, because if his brothers teased him by saying "yayow" he would get angry and retort, "No, *yayow!*"

One day when I came home from work, I found him sitting at the kitchen table singing, "Yellow, yellow, it is so easy to say yellow." Whatever the reason he had not been able pronounce *l*, he was able to overcome it, and, as all children do when they master a new skill or ability, he was playing with his new conquest.

Although most speech disorders are temporary, some may result from developmental delays. For example, some children may have a speech disorder related to hearing loss. Others may develop a lisp in response to stress. If the lisp persists after the child is eight years old, he or she should be seen by a speech therapist.

A child who lisps can be a target for teasing and bullying, so the disorder should be addressed as soon as it is obvious that it is not simply a developmental delay. Lisping is very remediable, and the treatment is usually short-term. No child needs to suffer the abuse that lisping can provoke.

There are no sure preventive measures that parents can take, but there are things that can be done to reduce the risk of a child developing a lisp. One way to lower the possibility of tongue thrusting is by restricting pacifier use to when it is really necessary—that is, when the child just needs to suck. Other measures with real benefits include speaking clearly when around the child and avoiding baby talk.

Additional practices include engaging children in exercises that help strengthen the mouth muscles. These include teaching children how to drink from a straw and to blow bubbles.

Reading to children and playing naming games with them helps children to develop good listening habits, which are essential not only for proper speech but for learning in general.

Lisping and other speech disorders due to delayed development go away with age for the vast majority of children. And speech therapy can help all but a few of those whose speech delays have other causes.

M

Manners and Morals

Many of our young visitors to Cape Cod in the summers often bring a friend along as company for their stay with us. I am always interested to observe the friends' behavior at the dinner table. For example, one of my granddaughter Lilly's friends will wait politely until everyone is served before picking up her knife or fork. She will also, at the end of the meal, politely ask to be excused from the table. In contrast, another of Lilly's friends will start to eat as soon as she is served, and will simply leave the table when she is done. I am tempted to say something to this young girl, but I don't want to embarrass her and make her feel uncomfortable. In the end, it is not the young girl's fault if her parents have not taught her how to behave at the dinner table.

Good manners are more than a formality. Children should be taught to be polite and to say "please," "thank you," "you're welcome," and "I'm sorry" when these are appropriate. Teaching young children good manners is important because they are the basis for all later moral behavior. When, at the dinner table, we wait for all to be served and seated before starting to eat, we are being considerate of others. The same is true when we use the words "please" and "thank you" and "excuse me." Consideration of others is at the heart of all moral behavior, starting from the Golden Rule, "Do unto others as you would have them do unto you." Learning good manners as a child is the foundation for responsible moral behavior as an adult.

Children learn best through imitation. That is why it is so important for us as adults to use them ourselves. As adults, we tend to think that children are generally like us in their thoughts but generally not like us in their feelings. In fact, just the reverse is true. Children are most like us in their feelings and least like us in their thoughts. Children feel deeply hurt if we break a promise and fail to say, "I am really sorry." They also feel bad when they are asked or told to do something without the adult using the words "please" and "thank you" when the child has done what was asked. Using good manners with children has the added benefit of making children feel good about themselves and about us as well.

In our hurried and hurrying society—where we eat 25 percent of our meals in our cars—table and other manners may seem old fashioned. But manners, and the moral values they reflect, are neither a fashion nor a trend nor a luxury; they are what make us human.

Mathematical Education, Early

An article titled "Studying Young Minds, and How to Teach Them," by Benedict Carey, was published in the *New York*

Times on December 21, 2009. It is very good example of very bad scientific reporting. The major problem with this article is that the author did not bother to research the subject he was writing about. He wrote, for example, "For much of the last century, educators and many scientists believed that children could not learn math at all before the age of five, that their brains simply were not ready."

Had the author bothered to look at a textbook in developmental or educational psychology, he would have found an extensive research literature on the numerical abilities of infants and young children. In addition, physician and educator Maria Montessori introduced a set of materials for teaching young children math concepts, such as size-graded colored sticks, and chains of ten beads that could be combined into larger decimal numbers. These materials are in widespread use today, and they help children move easily from simple to more complex math concepts.

Likewise, in 1952, Swiss psychologist Jean Piaget published *The Child's Conception of Number*, a comprehensive set of studies which detailed the development of the number concept. Piaget's book gave rise to a large number of studies dealing with various facets of children's early math abilities. Most of these studies have supported Piaget's description of the development of number through three stages. Nominal number (number as a name, like the number on a sports jersey) appears by the age of two. Ordinal number (ranking objects by size) is attained by the age of three or four. But integral number—the unit concept of number (necessary for doing numerical operations)—only appears at the age of five or six. Piaget's work has been incorporated into many preschool curricula, including the widely used HighScope curriculum, which is based on the principle that children learn best through hands-on experiences with people, materials, events, and ideas.

Yet Carey claimed that "the teaching of basic academic skills, until now largely the realm of tradition and guesswork, is giving way to approaches based on cognitive science." And: "In a typical preschool class children learn very little math."

Clearly, Carey has not visited many "typical" preschools, where all sorts of numerical activities, like counting, measuring, and classifying, are constantly going on. And many of the teaching techniques that Carey attributes to new findings from brain research, like cardinality (classifying objects) and one-to-one correspondence, are taken directly from Piaget.

And then there are simply flawed statements, such as: "by preschool, the brain can handle larger numbers and is struggling to link three crucial concepts. . . . " Whose brain is struggling? Children may struggle to link concepts, brains don't.

What is most disturbing about the article, besides its being published in the prestigious *New York Times*, is that it aids and abets those whose wish to push the grade school curriculum into the preschool. This has never worked in the past and will not work now. We really don't need the brain to tell us how best to teach young minds.

Mature Moms

The Center for Health Statistics reports that the number of women over forty who are having children has almost doubled from 20 percent in 1980 to 35 percent today. In many ways, this finding reflects the many changes in women's roles over the intervening decades, as well as improved health and increased longevity. But it also reflects changing lifestyles. With many more women pursuing full-time careers than was true in the past, child rearing is often put on hold until a career is well established. In addition, some couples want to take time for travel before they have children, who will keep them at home. It is also true that both men and women are marrying at a later age, and some couples may not marry until their late thirties. These and other considerations account for the increased number of new mature moms in our society.

Like most choices in life, the decision to have a child during the fourth or fifth decade of life has both risks and benefits. Mature mothers are at greater risk than are younger mothers of having a miscarriage or a child with a chromosomal abnormality such as Down syndrome. On the other hand, older mothers tend to be well educated, avid readers, and healthy eaters, and in good physical condition. In addition, mature mothers bring a greater self-confidence to their child rearing and are less influenced by parental peer pressure to engage in over-scheduling and over-programming. But they may be a little more likely than younger mothers to over-intellectualize their interactions with their young children.

Parenting always presents challenges, and those faced by mature moms are simply different from those younger moms confront. Not the least of these challenges is the unthinking comments of other parents. These range from mistaking the mature mom as the grandmother to asking whether the baby was an accident or achieved by in-vitro fertilization. A common question is "Aren't you tired?" Mature moms need to develop a thick skin.

On the other hand, the rewards for both mature moms and their children are great. Because the mature mom has a better-established sense of self, she is better able than a younger mom to distinguish between her own needs and those of her child. In addition, if a couple has been married for awhile, most of the issues as to who does what have been worked out, so they are not a source of parental conflict that can interfere with healthy child rearing.

The bottom line, from my point of view as a child psychologist, is, Does the new mature mom do a good job of parenting? And the answer to that question is overwhelmingly yes. And that is the only question, and the only answer, that really matters.

Military Children

According to the US Department of Defense there are currently 1.8 million children under the age of eighteen of US military personnel, 1,770,055 of whose parents are on active duty. Since 2001, as the death toll of fathers and mothers deployed to Iraq or Afghanistan has risen, so too has the number of military children in need of psychological counseling. Separation from one or both parents for long periods of time, worry about their safety, and often living away from a supportive kinship network can take its toll on children. The effect will depend on a number of factors, such as the child's age and sex, and the length of separation.

Infants and young children are perhaps least affected by the separation from one parent. At this age, children cannot really appreciate the reason for the separation, and it may be less traumatic if they are not already bonded to the absent parent. The separation is also made easier if there are older siblings who can help care for their younger brothers and sisters.

After the age of six or seven, however, children really miss the absent parent and have some sense that they may be in danger. It is helpful if the absent parent can communicate with the family on a weekly basis, either through the mail or the Internet. For elementary school children, the more communication with the absent parent the better. At this age, children are so needy of parents that they may be in denial of any danger or threat to the father or mother. It is best not to challenge this defense so long as it serves a useful purpose and the child is able to get on with his or her life.

For adolescents, an absent parent presents many challenges, but also opportunities to deal positively with the stress of separation and fear of parental death or injury. Many adolescents take on some of the responsibilities of the absent parent, and this gives them a sense of purpose and of being needed and useful. They also can share in taking care of their younger siblings. Giving adolescents increased responsibilities helps them to focus on the immediate needs of the family and siblings, and gives them less time to worry about the absent parent.

The child's sex plays a role to the extent that the child follows the cultural pattern where girls are expected to show their emotions while boys are not. This means that girls may be more willing to share their feelings than are boys. The length of separation is itself a factor. The longer the separation, the more difficult it is for the parent and the children to return to former patterns of family life. Family counseling is really important after long separations, particularly if the parent returns physically or psychologically injured.

Military children have a lot to cope with, but given constant communication and a supportive family and community, most are able to get on with their academic, social, and extracurricular lives.

Money, Educating Children About

This is a big topic, so I will make only a few of what, in my opinion, are the most important points. First, children learn best, and most easily, from the example set by parents. If you want your children to be responsible in money matters, you have to model responsible money management. In this regard, the first, and most important, example you can provide is to live within your means. This is important because it trains children to think about what is, and what is not, affordable. It also prevents the anxieties and stress associated with debt that are easily communicated to children.

Children can accept the fact that they may not be able to afford some of the things other children have if we set the example by the things we buy for ourselves. If you say, "I really would like to buy a new car but we can't afford it right now," your children can appreciate why they can not have, say, new bikes. But children do see, and do resent, the contradiction if you buy the new car and not the new bikes. Some parents sacrifice buying things they might like in order to buy things for their children. While this is admirable, the downside with this practice is that it may give children the wrong idea of the family income. It is much better to be realistic with children and for everyone to live at the level of what is affordable.

A second important point is to initiate children into the habit of saving at an early age. Piggy banks are a good starting point. Even young children can learn to start saving to buy something that is special to them. By the age of seven or eight, children can go with you to the bank to open a savings account. Children can deposit money they get from relatives, and at holidays, into the account. Looking at the bank book and seeing how much is in it is often reassuring to children. Again this money can be set aside for something the young person wants to buy but that might not be within the family budget. Learning to put money aside for future use is one of the most important money habits children can learn.

The question of allowances is a whole topic unto itself. In general, allowance should provide the child with sufficient money to meet reasonable weekly personal and social needs. An allowance should not be in exchange for doing chores, which are the child's responsibility as a family member. Rather, an allowance should be sufficient for the young person to enjoy an after-school soda or a snack along with his or her friends. Sometimes, an allowance should take into account the child's need to buy milk or other foods at the school cafeteria during lunch time. The amount of an allowance should be worked out in advance, taking account of the sort of needs outlined above, and renegotiated as the child grows older. If a child spends his or her allowance before the week is up, an advance should be made only if it is taken out of the next week's payment.

Helping children learn to handle money responsibly is one of the most important gifts we can give them.

Multiple Births

At a lecture engagement in Florida, I was introduced by a pediatrician who told me that she had two sets of twins. I did not have the chance to talk with her after the session because she had to return to her practice. One of the things I wanted to ask her was whether she had seen an increasing number of multiple births over her fifteen years as a practicing pediatrician. When I got home, I discovered a detailed report by the National Center for Health Statistics called "Trends in Twin and Triplet Births: 1980–97." The findings are quite remarkable. Over that time period, the number of twin births rose 52 percent (from 68,370 to 104,137) while the number of triplets and higher order multiple births climbed an astonishing 404 percent, (from 1,337 to 6,737). Birthrates of multiples were highest among women aged thirty and over. The older the mother, the greater the likelihood of her having multiple births. The rate was 63 percent for women aged forty to forty-four years of age and the rate rose to 1,000 percent for women forty-five to forty-nine years of age. Rates between non-Hispanic white and black mothers are now roughly comparable.

Accordingly, a great many parents are now facing the challenges of rearing twins and triplets, as well as higher order multiple births. Fortunately, there are now many books—such as *Raising Twins: What Parents Want to Know (and What Twins Want to Tell Them)*, by Eileen M. Pearlman and Jill Alison Ganon—and websites—such as Twins and Multiples at About. com and *American Baby Magazine:* Parenting Twins and Multiples at Parents.com—for parents raising twins and higher order multiple birth children.

Most of the experts, and parents of multiples, agree on a few basic requirements. Perhaps the most important one—a necessity—is to have family and friends help you, particularly during the early months. It is hard enough to meet all of the needs of one baby, much less two or more. It may be hard to do this if you are someone who prides herself on their independence and ability to meet all their responsibilities on her own. But some circumstances require that we put our pride aside, and multiple births is one of them. The areas in which you will probably need the most help are nights, going to the pediatrician, and doing the household chores, such as washing clothes and dishes, dressing, feeding, bathing, shopping, and so on. If you can afford to pay someone to help in these areas, that would make your life a lot easier. If you are not in that position, in most cases, family and friends are more than willing to pitch in.

A second requirement—a basic responsibility—is to appreciate that each baby is different. With twins, for example, even though one may be just a few minutes older than the other, it has been found that the older twin tends to be the most dominant. Getting to know each child's temperament and personality helps you better bond with each one and to treat him or her with the individuality he or she needs and deserves.

There are many more good ideas for parents of multiples in the sources mentioned above. The main thing to remember is that multiple birth children are a real challenge, but also a very real joy.

Music for Preemies

More than once I have questioned some of the purported long-term benefits of music lessons for children's mental development. A recent review of studies of using music in the care of premature infants, however, suggests that that music can have very positive immediate benefits for preterm infants. Researchers Tanya Pokki and Anne Kornhonen of the University of Oulu, Finland, analyzed a large number of studies dealing with the effect of music on premature infants. The title of their review is "The Effectiveness of Music on Pain in Premature Infants in the Neonatal Care Unit, a Systematic Review."

According to their report, neonatal units around the world are now using music on an informal basis as an adjunct to traditional medical procedures. Both parents and health professionals have the impression that it is beneficial for these infants. Music such as the famous lullaby by Johannes Brahms played to premature infants appears to induce behavioral changes such as calmer infants (and parents), more stable body functions, higher oxygen saturation, faster weight gain, and shorter hospital stays than is true for preemies who did not hear the music.

Another interesting finding is that listening to music also reduced the pain associated with the heel pricks used to obtain blood from these infants. Along the same lines, another study reported that playing lullabies and nursery rhymes lowered the pain levels that accompany circumcision. Pain levels were measured by heart rate and oxygen saturation; the rates for infants listening to music were indicative of a lower than expected pain experience.

Listening to music also seemed to ease the transition from feeding via nasal or gastric tubes to bottle feeding, with benefits both to the baby and to already overburdened health care professionals. Music not only eased the transition between feeding types but also increased the amount of food ingested. This music intervention has already been given its own name, the "pacifier-activated lullaby" system. Babies who had the lullaby music played to them had better feeding rates than did those who did not have the music played to them. This in turn increased body weight and made it possible for the babies to go home sooner.

As usual, some cautions are in order. the studies reviewed used small samples and were not always as rigorous as one might wish. Nonetheless, the consistency of the findings across studies and the increased use of music in neonatal wards suggest that playing lullabies and nursery rhymes can indeed have many immediate positive benefits for premature infants, for their parents, and for the health care system.

N

Naps, The Importance Of

Sleeping and napping are vitally important for an infant. An infant's brain and body are growing at a very rapid rate, and such growth requires the slow metabolic rate provided by sleeping and napping. Daytime napping follows a typical course that nonetheless can vary from baby to baby. During the first two months of life, most babies will sleep for three- or four-hour periods during the day and night. There is no clear pattern to this sleeping and napping and you are best advised to simply adapt to your baby's own timetable. As the speed of brain and body growth eases a bit by the third or fourth month, your baby may begin to show a more regular nap pattern.

At about six months, your baby will probably take three naps a day, one in the morning and two in the afternoon. By the end of first year, most infants are down to two solid naps a day, one in the morning and one in the afternoon.

When your baby begins to show a more predictable nap pattern, at about three or four months, you can begin to help set a nap schedule. To do this, you need to learn the signals your baby gives that nap time is in the offing. You can use these signals to help you shape a regular nap schedule. These signals include restlessness and/or eye rubbing at midmorning or after a meal. If you keep a record of the time the sleep signals show up, you can anticipate them and put the baby down ten or fifteen minutes before the sleep signals usually appear. Prepare for naptime by engaging in quiet activities just before putting him or her down. As the baby gets older and sleeps less, you can still use the sleep signals to set up a less frequent nap schedule. While consistency is important, it is usually impossible to keep the same schedule every day. That is really not a problem as long as you stick to the overall pattern most of the time.

Here are couple of other suggestions. It is helpful if you can put your baby in his or her crib to nap, where he or she is used to sleeping. You really don't have to change him or her into pajamas, but make sure whatever your baby is wearing is loose and comfortable. Finally, all babies are different, but if you tune in to your baby's sleep signals and build your activities around them, you have the best chance of having a baby with a predictable nap schedule.

Nature and Nurture

The bicentennial of the birth of Charles Darwin suggested an entry on the role of nature and nurture on the development of the infant and young child. Many traits are genetic. For example, a baby's eye and hair color are clearly genetically linked. So too are body build and relative height. Because an infant gets half of his or her genes from the mother and half from the father, it is hard to predict which traits will come from whom. That is why children from the same parents can look and behave so differently.

Other traits reflect some combination of both heredity and environment. An infant who has a predisposition to asthma, for example, may develop asthma in Massachusetts but not in Arizona.

The matching of predispositions with environment also occurs across historical changes in the environment. A child who has a predisposition for technologies such as computers would have had no outlet for that predisposition had he or she been born in the nineteenth century. Likewise, a child today who has a predisposition for hand crafts might find it harder now than in previous centuries to find a suitable venue to work in.

Disentangling what comes from nature and what from nurture is perhaps the most difficult when it comes to psychological traits. One of the most interesting types of research in this regard is that of identical twins. Inasmuch as they share exactly the same heredity, any differences should be attributable to the environment.

Investigators at the University of Minnesota have conducted longitudinal studies of twins raised both together and apart with interesting results. They compared siblings who were separated at birth and reared in different families with twins who had been raised in the same family. They found that the twins who had been raised apart were as likely as those raised together to be similar in personality traits such as interests and attitudes. In the case of identical twins, nature trumps nurture. The same conclusion can be drawn from a comparison of an adopted twin with his or her adopted parents and siblings. The investigators found that while such children may have certain superficial behavior or other traits activated by certain environmental factors, they were still more like their twins when it came to more basic traits like the IQ.

Certainly, environment plays a role in determining such traits as IQ and some personality variables. But it is clear from these studies that environment can do only so much. This research should give caution to those who argue that one or another educational scheme will raise a child's IQ. For children who have not been environmentally deprived, this is simply not possible.

Night Terrors

When your three-year-old wakes you up in the middle of the night with a cry like, "Mommy! Mommy! There's a bear in my room!" what do you do?

Cries like this are only heard after the child acquires what Jean Piaget called the "symbolic function," the ability to create symbols. This usually appears after the second year, when the child is well into language. A young child who holds up a potato chip and says, "Look, Mommy—a butterfly," has created a symbol for a butterfly. Dreams require symbol formation, and that is why night terrors appear only after a child has reached this stage. As in this example, the night terror usually involves what the child has recently seen or heard (in real life, or in a book, or on TV).

Given that the child is now able to create dream symbols, how to you deal with night terrors? There are several possibilities. You might, for example, take the factual approach. You might go into your child's room, turn on all the lights, and then say, "I am going to search for the bear and see if I can find him. I am looking under the bed—no bear there. I am looking in the closet—nope, no bear there. Now I am looking in your toy chest—nope, no bears there. I guess the bear is gone now." You kiss your child and say, "Good night, honey. The bear has gone away." It usually takes only a short time, however, for the bear to return and for the cry to be repeated.

Alternatively, you might take a more sympathetic approach. After turning on the lights, you might say, "Oh, I see the bear. What a nice bear! He likes me to pet him on his head. He is really a very friendly bear, but now he tells me that it is time for him to go to bed, so he is going. Good-bye, bear. Sleep tight." When you look back at your child, you may find that he or she is looking at you as if you had suddenly gone off your rocker. After saying good night and leaving the room, the bear returns and the child cries, "Mommy! Mommy! The bear is back!"

A third approach is to bypass the bear issue and respond to the child's feelings—what the night terror is really all about. This is the approach advocated by the late Israeli psychologist Haim Ginott, author of the bestselling book *Between Parent and Child*, who advocated for accepting the child's feelings and responding to them. Using this approach, you might give your child a hug and say, "Your daddy and I love you very much and we are not going to let anything or anybody hurt you." The trick here, in opposition to the other two approaches, is to neither deny nor accept the child's reality. When we accept or deny the child's reality, we only entrench the child in his or her position. By not denying or accepting the child's reality, but responding only to the child's feelings, we bypass the question of the bear's reality. We thus avoid the resistance created by trying to deal with that issue.

Neither denying nor accepting a child's reality when it is different from your own is an effective way of avoiding a lot of needless debate and argument.

Noisy Little Children

We often have four little children, all girls, spend a week with us over the Fourth of July holiday. When they arrive, I am reminded of how much little children love noise—any noise. They like to yell, to scream, to cry, to talk a blue streak. Vocal chords are only a part of the din, however. Once, one of our little guests found a pint-sized kazoo (how in the world did I miss that in the preparation for their arrival?) which she happily tooted—ad infinitum, it seemed. But little children also create their own noisemakers—anything that can be banged will be banged, and anything that can be rattled will be rattled. And there are endless toys that have an Energizer Bunny to keep them running—endlessly playing their tunes, singing their songs, and simply adding to the cacophony that reverberates through our once-quiet home.

As a psychologist, I cannot allow a behavioral observation to be recorded without making some attempts to explain the phenomenon.

I believe that Freud was correct when he argued that most of human behavior is over-determined, that is, due to multiple causes. Young children's love of noise and noisemaking falls within this category.

There is, first of all, the neurological cause. Young children's sensory systems are quite new and in the process of development. Perhaps they need noise, in part at least, to stimulate and nourish the auditory centers of the brain.

There are a number of psychological explanations as well. When little children make noise, they make adults take notice. So one of the functions of noisemaking is to draw attention to the noisemaker.

Another reason may be the "whistling in the dark" syndrome, in which making noise is a way of dealing with fear and anxiety. If you make enough noise, loud enough and long enough, perhaps the dreaded monster will go away. And we must never forget the nuisance factor. Once children discover that adults don't like all the noise, they make it to get back at us. After all, we are big and all-powerful, and they are small and have few weapons to fight back with. But noise happens to be one of them. Also, making noise is a passive-aggressive maneuver.

Making noise is what young children do, and they can't be blamed for it.

There are probably sociological reasons as well. Noisemaking may be a unifying activity for young children. In making noise together, they join forces and find common cause—against the silence-loving adult world. Indeed, noisemaking may be the universal language of young children which children all over the world use and understand without translation. "Infants and young children of the world unite, let us all make noise together!"

Now that I have a better understanding of the many reasons why young children love noise and love making it, I should be more accepting and understanding of this behavior. And of course I am, but as much as I enjoy their stays, I look forward to the quiet when the week is over.

Nursing Styles, Infant

Breastfeeding is never as simple and straightforward as it might seem. Indeed, Edith Jackson, a pediatrician at Yale described the five nursing styles below in the 1950s. Knowing a baby's style helps you know how to respond appropriately.

Barracuda

These babies know what they are after, and they grab the breast and suck vigorously for ten to twenty minutes. They are sometimes called "little vacuums." It is important for these babies to be firmly and comfortably attached. In their eagerness, some barracudas may latch on in a way that causes pain. If this happens it is best to detach the baby and start over until the fit is comfortable for you both.

Excited

These babies are impulsive. In their eagerness to feed, they grab the nipple with their mouths but then may lose it and cry out in frustration. It makes sense to try and anticipate when these babies will want to nurse. This sometimes occurs when the baby gets up from a nap or tries to suck its thumb. You can help the baby by making feeding a priority and doing it in a comfortable setting. The movement of a rocking chair can sometimes help.

Procrastinator

These "lazy" eaters don't seem to want to go to the trouble during the first few days after birth. Even when they cry for the breast, they may stop nursing after a quick suck or two. Although these babies may seem easy, sleeping a lot and crying less, they need a lot of attention. You have to try and feed them every hour. Even if the baby does not seem to be getting enough, though, he or she may be getting enough. The baby's weight is a good index. All babies lose weight in the first few days after birth, but should regain at least birth weight in about ten days.

Gourmet

Like all gourmets, these babies like to taste their food in advance. Such babies play with the nipple and taste the milk before they begin sucking in earnest. Once they find it to their liking, they nurse well. As with barracudas, it is important that the bite is right and not painful; it is okay to detach the baby to get a more comfortable fit. Like all gourmets, these babies may give evidence of really enjoying their meal.

Resters

Resters are not likely to ever get fat. Like most thin people, they do not rush their meal, and they take rests between each mouthful. Sometimes they fall asleep during nursing and wake up wanting to pick up where they left off. Don't be misled by the rester into thinking he or she is not getting enough from that particular breast. Let your own sense of the fullness of your breasts, rather than the baby's eating pattern, be your guide. These babies can't really be hurried, and you just have to resign yourself to the time it takes to feed them. The one-on-one time with your baby is very important to your relationship, so take the time and enjoy it.

O

Only Children

More than a century has passed since G. Stanley Hall, founder of Clark University, declared that "being an only child is a disease in itself." Such negative images of only children are being reignited by the current youth problems in China resulting from the government's "one child" policy. But China is a special case because it is a forced rather than a voluntary choice. Today, there is a growing body of research evidence that refutes many of the long-held misconceptions regarding only children.

In her book, *The Case for the Only Child*, Susan Newman does a good job of undoing many of our pre-conceived ideas about the selfishness of single-child parents and the negative effects of being an only child. With regard to selfishness, Newman argues that there are many socio-economic factors pushing parents to have only one child. Couples are marrying later, mothers are older, and there is real concern about the cost of raising and educating more than one child. Thanks to these factors, single-child families are increasing at a faster rate than multi-child families and are becoming the norm.

And the data support her claim. The nuclear family image of a mother, father, and two or three children has given way to a more contemporary picture. Government reports indicate that the birthrate in America reached its highest point of 3.7 children per family in 1980. Today the birthrate is about 1.88, and some 20 percent of women have only one child. Is it really selfishness to worry about whether you can afford to give your child a college education at today's prices?

And there is increasing evidence to show that being an only child can have real advantages over a child with siblings. Researcher Douglas Downey of Ohio State University reports data about the social competence of only children vis-à-vis those with siblings. He found that by seventh grade, only children were as popular with their peers as were children with siblings. In a larger-scale study, Downey also found that only children do better than children with siblings academically.

Downey's findings were supported by the work of Heidi Riggio of California State College, who found that it was not possible to tell the difference between adult singletons, and adults from multi-child families with respect to social competence, making friends, and comfort in new social situations.

Likewise, Jeffrey Kluger, in his book, *The Sibling Effect: What the Bonds Among Brothers and Sisters Reveal About Us* concedes that there are benefits to being an only child. "Only children tend to wind up with a better vocabulary and a more sophisticated sense of humor, simply because they grow up in a house outnumbered by parents."

So the general consensus today is that the increase in single-child families is largely determined by socio-economic changes in our society. Likewise, it is generally agreed today that only children fare no worse than children from multi-child families, and may actually fare better. There is now a website dedicated to only children, and many participants on the site offer their own case histories as evidence that they were not harmed by being an only child.

Over-Parenting, Overcoming

In a recent TIME Magazine article, Nancy Gibbs describes what she calls "The Growing Backlash Against Overparenting." Gibbs argues that the book *Free Range Kids: How to Raise Safe Self-Reliant Children* is but one of many kinds of parental revolts against hyper-parenting, which include "slow" parenting and "simplicity" parenting. The themes of the backlash include the ideas that less is more, that hovering is dangerous, and that failure is fruitful. She summarizes the heart of the revolt in this way: "You really want your children to succeed? Learn when to leave them alone. When you lighten up they will fly higher. We're often the ones who hold them down."

Ironically, the recession helped to stimulate the over-parenting revolt. Gibbs cites a CBS poll which found that a third of parents have cut their children's extracurricular activities. These parents not only cut back, they downsized, simplifying their lives and spending more time with their children—rather than shipping them off to lessons or putting them in organized sports. And they found that they really like the new arrangement. Although Gibbs claims that parents are finally waking up to the fact that over-protecting and over-scheduling is doing more harm than good to both themselves and to their children, a 2009 *New York Times* poll found that many out-of-work

parents found that joblessness "poisoned" all their relationships. So, while it may have some benefits, its negative effects
probably still outweigh the positives.

With respect to pushing children too hard to grow up too
fast, I published *The Hurried Child* more that a quarter century
ago. And we are seeing the long-term results of that strategy.
Gibbs describes high school teachers who received text messages from parents protesting an exam grade even before the
class is over. College deans describe many of today's freshmen
as "crispies," who arrive at college already burnt out. I have
met with headmasters of exclusive private schools who tell me
that when a child is in trouble, they don't see the parents, but
rather the family lawyer.

As academics, my colleagues and I have little chance against
the multi-million dollar advertising budgets of the many companies that feed over-parenting to sell products. It is really fascinating that it is taking a major recession to wake parents up
to the craziness of over-parenting. I guess good can come from
bad. For parents who want support for combating parental peer
pressure to over-program and over-schedule, Gibbs suggests
going to the many websites where parents can confess, confide,
and confirm their own experiences with over-parenting. Maybe
at last the fog is lifting over child rearing.

P

Parent Nostalgia

It is easy to mythologize our own childhood and to compare it unfavorably with the way children live today. In fact, of course, the nostalgia is not so much for a lost era in history as it is for a lost time in our personal past, when we were young, healthy, and relatively stress free.

I was reminded of this personal nostalgia when I read Erik Kolbell's article "Fake Nostalgia for a Pre-Therapy Past" in the *New York Times* in which he told of a man at a bar putting down the readiness we have today to provide treatment for children with mental, emotional, and behavioral problems. The man claimed that his generation was made of much sterner stuff. The author, himself a victim of what we now call ADHD, wonders how far he might have gone had his disability been recognized and treated as is being done today.

While it is true that we have lost some benefits of the past, particularly the socializing influence of the culture of childhood, it is also true that we have gained a great deal in the way of provisions for children with special needs and disabilities.

My granddaughter is a case in point. She has Down syndrome. Hardly more than a half century ago there would have been little or no help for her parents, who would have had to take on most of the responsibility for her physical and mental development. Schools sometimes accepted such children, but often shunted them aside into "special" classrooms. That was the fate of one my grandnieces, now in her forties, who also has Down syndrome. Her parents had full responsibility for her early development and education.

In contrast, my granddaughter Maya has had community provided in-service educators visiting her twice a week since soon after she was born. They helped my son and daughter-in-law give Maya the appropriate physical and mental exercises needed to maximize her somewhat limited abilities. This continued for three years.

She is now in a public kindergarten, loves to swim, ride horses, and zooms around on her tricycle. I had the thrill of a lifetime when she sang "Happy Birthday" to me over the phone clearly and in tune. I am sure she would never have made this progress without the help her parents received, thanks to the new legislation for children with special needs. I am sure there are many stories like hers.

So it is easy to lament the loss of many of the good things about our own time growing up, and to be critical of the child rearing practices of today. But it has been said that a society can be judged by the manner in which treats its children with special needs. In that respect, at least, our contemporary society scores much higher than it did in the past.

Parent Stress

In everyday usage, "stress" refers to our reactions to an extraordinary demand for adaptation. Our bodies are programmed for these extraordinary demands. When they occur, our heart rate and blood pressure increase, and adrenalin flows through our system. These reactions give us the needed additional energy to cope with the situation.

Every parent of a young infant is stressed because the need to awake every three or four hours to feed the baby is an extraordinary demand. The reaction is often tiredness, headaches, and body aches, as well as ill humor.

Stress and stress reactions have to do with our energy resources. An analogy would be our savings and checking accounts. We use the energy in our checking accounts to deal with everyday demands, such as going to work, meeting with friends, exercising, etc. We replenish our checking account energy with food and sleep much as we replenish our bank checking account with a weekly or monthly paycheck. Our savings account energy is what we keep in reserve for emergencies. In part, it is genetic and has to do with our heredity.

In the example above, the parent has to call on energy reserves in order to meet the demands of infant care. In most cases, as the baby grows older and sleeps through the night, the parent's stress symptoms usually disappear. But the demands of infant care are only some of the stressors faced by parents. Stressors will change as the child matures. That is why it is so important to find ways to deal with stress effectively. One thing I have found with parents, particularly with mothers, is that they feel guilty if they take any time for themselves. But taking time—for meeting with friends or having dinner out with a spouse—is not selfish. It is necessary for replenishing the resources you need to function effectively as a parent.

Parent Warfare

It is a generally accepted premise among family counselors that parents should not fight in front of their children whatever their age. The reasoning for this is straightforward. Young children are egocentric, and when they see their parents fight, they feel it is because of something they did. School-age children construct the idea of the "good parent" and tend to deny anything bad about them, at least to others. When they see the parents fight, this overturns their belief in parental goodness. Adolescents, who are just forming their own romantic relationships, worry about whether they will end up unhappy with their romantic choice. And, given how common divorce has become, children at all ages wonder whether the fight is a prelude to that eventuality.

So we shouldn't fight in front of the kids, period. Well, on the other hand . . .

Most of the research and clinical experience leading to the foregoing rule was based on the assumption of heated battles. A recent study by researchers at the University of Rochester concluded that it is the *nature* of the conflict that will determine its positive or negative effect upon the children.

The study, described in an article called "Constructive and Destructive Marital Conflict: Emotional Security and Children's Pro-social Behavior" involved 235 families with children between the ages of five and seven. It was a three-year study during which parents described their argument style and that of their spouse. The researchers also videotaped couples coping with a difficult issue and rated the interactions as "constructive" or "destructive."

By "constructive conflict" the researchers meant that the partners showed mutual respect and affection for one another and engaged in problem solving in a supportive way. "Destructive conflict," on the other hand was described as hostile, angry, and involving behavior such as physical and verbal aggression, threat, and personal insult.

One finding of the study was a strong relationship between parental use of constructive conflict and their children's positive social adjustment. The authors suggested that emotional security was the underlying link between parental conflict and social adjustment. Parents who conflicted in a constructive way fostered the child's sense of emotional security. And it is likely that parents who engage in constructive parenting are warm, accepting, and respectful with their children. Destructive parenting, in contrast, was related to children's poor social adjustment, emotional insecurity, and behavior problems.

This study illustrates that the type of parental conflict is another of the many evidences of a healthy or unhealthy marital relationship. Put differently, constructive conflict within a happy marriage contributes to children's emotional security and social well-being. Destructive conflict within an unhappy marriage can have just the opposite effect.

Perhaps that is what Leo Tolstoy had in mind when he wrote that "All happy families are alike; all unhappy families are unhappy in their own way."

Parenting, The Basic Rule Of

How much should we try to protect our children from life's vi-cissitudes? Some parents feel that it is their job to protect their children from teasing, bullying, and fighting. These parents believe that their failure to do so will undermine the child's self-esteem and ability to succeed in life. Other parents feel just the opposite and contend that their children will learn in-dependence, resiliency, and strength only from dealing with adversity.

Both positions have merit, and it is only when taken to ex-tremes that they do harm. Neither over-protection nor under-protection from hardship will be of benefit to the majority of children.

More significantly, both positions leave out the all-important variable: the child. The same boiling water that hardens the egg softens the carrot, and the same experience that strengthens one child may devastate another. This is true even if both children are from the same family. Children are different, and there is simply no one parenting style of that fits all of them. The sim-plest and most obvious example is, of course, the difference between the rearing of boys and the rearing of girls.

There is no one best style of parenting, but there is one ba-sic rule of child rearing. It is a fundamental rule that holds for other areas of life as well. In business, the rule is to keep your eyes on the store. In sports, the rule is to keep your eyes on the ball. In child rearing, the rule is to keep your eyes on the child.

We all know our children better than anyone else. Most of us can estimate our children's IQs within ten points. Reflecting upon and using what we know about our children is the surest and best guide to parenting them effectively and appropriately.

Parenting Fads

Over the years, any number of weird child rearing ideas have been introduced, claiming special benefits from particular practices or products. Most commonly, these proposals come from entrepreneurs trying to sell books, toys, DVDs, or some combination of these. In most cases, they have little or no research to back up their claims. But sometimes these ideas have benefits for children quite different from those that were promised.

For example, proponents of the "Mozart effect" claimed that playing Mozart to infants and young children increased their intelligence and overall mental acuity. While this claim has never been supported by research, playing Mozart to premature infants *has* been found to be very beneficial in quieting them and making them more tolerant of medial procedures. So some practices proposed for one effect may have unintended positive consequences for another.

That was my reaction on reading about New Zealand child expert Polly Elam's organization Resources for Infant Educarers. According to Elam, parents should be treating babies and toddlers with more respect. In practice, this means talking to infants as if they were adults and not putting them in high chairs, car seats, or allowing them to play with the most popular child toys.

In addition, she argues that parents should also ask the baby before ministering to them. Parents should ask the baby's permission before picking him or her up, changing a diaper, or taking the baby shopping or on an outing. This means that parents are expected to tell the infant what you, the parent, are about to do, and to wait for the infant's response. If parents fail to consult with their infant in this way, they should apologize to the baby and tell him or her that they did not act properly.

According to Elam, these practices lead to happy infants who are problem solvers and who have high self-esteem. Her key message is that parents need to slow their pace and give their infants a chance to respond and to solve their own problems.

Another example she provides is waving good-bye to the baby. According to Elam, parents often do not wait long enough for the child to wave back. In her view, parents should not leave until the baby waves back. She says her program is all about respecting the baby and allowing an infant to grow at his or her own pace. The program has taken hold in California and New Zealand. There is a financial cost; parents who attend the RIE workshop to learn the system pay $125 for the privilege.

On the face of it, the program has little to recommend it. Infants do not understand adult language, so telling them what you are going to do and asking their permission makes no sense. Again, the claim that such practices enhance self-esteem and problem solving has little or no factual support. Indeed, the child does not have a sense of self until after the age of two. And how is the infant to respond to the request before he or she has language? And if it could, what if the baby says, "No, don't change my diaper"? If the baby doesn't wave back, do the parents never leave?

On the other hand, talking to the baby while ministering to him or her is comforting to the child and provides a rich language environment. If that talk describes what the parent is doing to the infant, that is simply another mode of talk and is all to the good. But there is no point to asking the baby's permission. Certainly we have to respect the baby's timing, but we also have to help the baby learn routines an infant cannot learn on his or her own.

So talking to a baby and telling the infant what you are about to do is a healthy practice that places the activity in a communication framework. But asking a baby's permission and apologizing to an infant for not asking is a bit over the top.

Parenting, Some Wrong Ideas About

In their recent book, *Nurtureshock: New Thinking about Children*, Po Bronson and Ashley Merryman use abundant research evidence to show how mistaken and misguided is much of our conventional wisdom regarding child rearing. The book is written in an engaging and sympathetic style that is friendly toward, rather than critical of, parents. These authors appreciate that parents are not to blame if accepted ideas, or those of professed child rearing experts, turn out to be wrong.

I am pleased to say that a number of the erroneous ideas Bronson and Merryman describe are also dealt with in *Parenting on the Go: Birth to Six, A to Z.* For example, they show that second language learning in early childhood is less than useless (see the entry "Second Languages, Learning"). And they call attention to what they call the "two basic errors of thinking about children." One is the parental belief that what is true for adults is true for children. A number of entries in *Parenting on the Go* deal with this issue, including "Instructing Young Children, Tips On" and "Questions, Children's."

But there are also many wrong ideas that I haven't touched on. For example, the idea that children and adolescents can function well with less than eight to ten hours of sleep is simply wrong. Bronson and Merryman cite data to the effect that children and adolescents sleep at least an hour less today than they did in the past. Recent brain research shows that too little sleep can impair memory. Another wrong assumption is that children who attend racially diverse schools will be more tolerant and have racially diverse friendships. In fact, if anything, racially diverse schools can contribute to prejudice. Another interesting misconception is that involved fathers—those who spend a lot of time caring for their children—will do a better job of child rearing. In fact, many of these fathers, perhaps because of their closeness to their children, are unwilling to engage in the necessary discipline.

There are many more gems in this book, and it is a fun read.

Parenting Styles

A number of year ago, psychologist Diana Baumrind described in two articles ("Raising Competent Children" and "The Influence of Parenting Style on Adolescent Competence and Substance Use") four parenting styles that have different child behavior outcomes. Additional research has provided ample evidence for the validity of these styles and their long-lasting effects upon children's overall development.

Although the described styles are generalizations that never fit any family exactly, they provide useful reference points for parents to assess their own parenting practices. The styles are defined by the extent to which parents rank high or low in terms of "demandingness" and "responsiveness."

"Permissive" parents are those who rank low on demandingness but high on responsiveness. These parents tend to be lenient, do not demand mature behavior, and permit a lot of self-regulation. They also try to avoid confrontation. At the same time, these parents are loving and supportive without

P

175

being demanding. Children who have "permissive" parents are not likely to be involved in problem behavior. They do average work in school but do have high self-esteem, good social skills, and show few signs of depression.

"Authoritarian" parents tend to be very demanding but relatively low in responsiveness. These parents are very concerned with obedience and social status. Such parents do not provide explanations for their rules and do not expect to be challenged. Although they provide a well-structured environment, they tend to provide little emotional warmth and support. Children who come from "authoritarian" homes tend to perform moderately in school and not to be involved in problem behavior. But these children also have poor social skills, low self-esteem, and high levels of depression.

"Authoritative" parents are both demanding and responsive. Such parents are often described as "setting limits with love." Although they monitor their children's behavior, they do so in a non-intrusive way. In disciplining their children, they are supportive rather than punitive, and offer rewards for good behavior rather than punishment for bad. They have clear goals for their children and want them to be both self-assertive and socially responsible. Children from "authoritative" homes are likely to do well in school and to be socially and vocationally competent, with high self-esteem and low rates of depression.

"Uninvolved" parents rank low in both demandingness and responsiveness. At the extreme, such parents may be rejecting and neglectful. But most parents in this category are, fortunately, not at the extreme. Children who come from homes with "uninvolved" parents tend not to do well in school, to be involved in problem behavior, to have poor social skills, to have low self-esteem, and to be subject to depression.

Like all research findings, the effects of different styles of parenting are generalizations and may not hold for all families and children. In addition, it is important to say that the reality is that all parents probably engage in all four parenting styles at times. What is important is that, as much as possible, parents strive toward the "authoritative" style, which is the most supportive of healthy overall child development.

Parenting Styles, Conflicting

One of the ways to describe different parenting styles comes from famed sociologist Erving Goffman, who called them "frames." For Goffman, frames are repetitive social situations with their own rules, expectations, and understandings. These social realities are often learned early and may remain more or less unconscious until we interact with someone who has a conflicting frame. This often happens after a couple marries.

Consider the following scenario. A young man growing up in a well-to-do suburb has a mother who does everything for him. Each morning he finds his bureau drawers filled with clean socks, underwear, and freshly ironed shirts. In the kitchen he finds a well-prepared breakfast ready and waiting for him, and his lunch neatly packed in a brown paper bag. When he gets back from school, he has his milk and cookies and goes out to play. That is his reality, and his idea about what women—mothers—do.

In the same neighborhood, a young woman with the same socio-economic level and same ethnic and racial background is growing up with a different reality. Both her parents work, and she has to look after her own clothes and get her own breakfast. After school she may put the clothes in the washing machine and get some things ready for dinner. In this family, everybody just does what need to be done. That is her reality.

Imagine, now, that when they grow up these two young people meet, date, and fall in love. They decide to marry once they finish college—which they then proceed to do. After they return from the honeymoon, they set up housekeeping in a small apartment.

The first morning, the husband is ready to go off to his new job, but he is distressed to find he has no clean socks, underwear, or freshly pressed shirts. In the kitchen there is no breakfast or lunch waiting. Frustrated and unhappy, he complains to his wife, "Where are my clean clothes, my breakfast, and my lunch? My mother. . . . " To which his wife replies, "Don't be such a baby, learn to do your own laundry and to cook."

When there is a conflict of social realities, we have the tendency to attribute bad motives to those who don't share our view of the world. This is true of married couples as well. In the above example, the husband is likely to accuse the wife of not caring about his welfare. The wife, in turn, is likely to accuse her husband of being spoiled and self-centered. Other frame conflicts may center on gift giving (a big deal in some families, not in others), bathroom etiquette (I leave this to your imagination), or how to celebrate holidays and birthdays.

When a couple has children, frame conflicts often arise with respect to child rearing practices. To illustrate, if one parent was brought up in a home where children were given a great deal of freedom and the other parent in a home where there were strict rules and obligations, this can cause a frame conflict. The tendency to see the other parent's reality as stemming from bad motives can make the situation worse.

For example, a father may accuse the mother of being unwilling to take the time or make the effort to discipline. And the mother may claim that the father is more concerned about keeping the house clean and neat than about the well-being of the children. In such disputes, children are caught in the middle.

As a family counselor, I found that such conflicts can be resolved if the relationship is healthy in other respects. I tell my clients something like this: "The best way of dealing with conflicting realities is for each of you to talk a little bit about the way you have been brought up. In this way, each of you can appreciate that it is upbringing, rather than bad intentions, which is the root of the conflict. If you can accept such differences as such—as simply differences—then you can proceed to a rational discussion as how to resolve the dispute."

In the above example, it is usually possible to find a compromise between freedom and regulation if each parent is willing to give a little. It should be said, however, that sometimes differences between parents stem more from personality clashes than from learned frames. Personality is harder to change, and for such clashes the relationship can last only if the parents make the effort to adapt to, rather than to try and change, the others' behavior patterns. It is much easier to change frames than it is to alter personality.

Parents, Gourmet

A few years ago a *Wall Street Journal* article called "The Trophy Kids Go to Work" caught my attention and I filed it for future reference. The article gives examples of how some of the current crop of college graduates is approaching the workplace.

The author, Ron Alsop, writes: "Although members of other generations were considered somewhat spoiled in their youth, millennials feel an unusually strong sense of entitlement. Older adults criticize the high-maintenance rookies for demanding too much too soon. 'They want to be CEO tomorrow,' is a common refrain from corporate recruiters."

The article was particularly interesting to me because of something I wrote more than twenty years ago when these graduates were in kindergarten. In my book *Miseducation: Preschoolers at Risk*, I described a number of parenting styles and their consequences. One of these styles was most characteristic of newly affluent parents whom I described as "Gourmet" parents: Many older wealthy families have learned to instill a sense of public service in their offspring. But many newly affluent middle-class parents have not acquired this talent. We are using our children as symbols of leisure-class standing without building in the safeguards against an overweening sense of entitlement—a sense of entitlement that may incline some young people more toward the good life than toward the hard work that, for most of us, makes the good life possible.

That is to say, the outcome of Gourmet parenting was predictable. Children were given the best of everything, without anything being required on their part. As a result, they were less than appreciative of what they were given but got angry if they did not receive what they believed to be their due. They have carried these attitudes with them into adulthood.

The important point is that what we do as parents plays an important role in shaping the personalities of our children. In *Miseducation* I also describe "Milk and Cookie" parents, who want their children to succeed and do well, but who also want, and try to give them, a happy childhood. They try to provide their children with the time and opportunity to be children and to engage in self-initiated, age-appropriate, play and games. In such play they learn mutual respect—for example, following the rules their peers make but also expecting their peers to follow the rules they have devised. Mutual respect tempers any tendency toward entitlement and the sense of being special. Many of my most well-rounded and grounded college students were reared by Milk and Cookie parents.

As parents, we all want our children to do well and to succeed in their personal and occupational lives. The problem with Gourmet parents is that they confuse what they would like for their children with what the children would like for themselves.

Q

Questions, Answering Children's

Once, we took our granddaughter Heather to the beach for an outing when she was four years old. She was having a grand time making sand balls and running in and out of the water, chased by waves. When we settled down to have our lunch, she looked up at the warm sun and asked, "Papa, what makes the sun shine?"

I could, of course, have given her the scientific answer about the relation of heat and light, but I know that would have gone over her head. I recalled that Jean Piaget, the famed Swiss psychologist, noted that young children believe everything has a purpose. So I replied to Heather's question by saying, "The sun shines to keep us warm and to help flowers grow." She was perfectly happy with that response.

Alternatively, I could have asked her what she believed. Most children have their own answers to the questions they ask, and are perfectly happy to share them with us. But if we employ this strategy, we really have to listen to what they say, and to take them seriously even if their response seems silly or nonsensical to us.

Young children simply think about the world a bit differently than we do. Their perspective is not wrong, because all children of four or five think this way. It is an age-appropriate mode of thought. It is only when we look at it from the viewpoint of adult logic that it appears faulty. This is a very important point. Too often I find parents so eager to give the child the "right" answer that they miss the child's intent. This leaves the child feeling frustrated and misunderstood. It may also make the child reluctant to display curiosity.

The young child's questions are an opportunity to build patterns of communication that are essential for healthy interactions as the child matures. Some parents fear that giving the child the "wrong" answer is not a good teaching strategy. I don't agree. In the first place, saying, for example, that the sun shines to keep us warm, or that rain falls to make the flowers grow, is not really wrong—the sun does keep us warm, and the rain does make the flowers grow.

More importantly, as children develop they will spontaneously give up their earlier modes of thought. For example, when children who once believed in fairy tales, Santa Claus, and the tooth fairy get older, they take great pride, in saying, "I don't believe in that anymore." Giving up earlier modes of thought is an important marker of emerging maturity, and children appreciate our understanding and support of that progression.

R

Reading, Teaching Babies

The term "reading" suggests that the activity is a singular skill, when in fact it is the culmination of many different developmental achievements. For example, reading is in part a visual skill in that it involves the ability to recognize letters and words. It also involves the muscular control that allows the child to explore a page from left to right and from top to bottom. It is also an auditory skill that requires the child to distinguish the basic sounds of his or her native language and eventually to begin to associate these sounds with the printed word. Last but not least, reading is a cognitive skill because it requires understanding and interpretation.

The research on reading is quite abundant and quite consistent in demonstrating the age at which formal instruction in reading (namely phonics) should be introduced. Formal instruction in reading is more effectively introduced between the ages of five and seven, by which time most children have acquired the ability to listen, to understand, and to follow rules.

This is true because it takes years for children to acquire the many pre-reading skills required to profit from formal reading instruction. Cross-cultural research dramatically illustrates the results of different approaches to teaching reading. In Scandinavian countries and in Russia, reading is usually not taught until the age of six or seven. Children in these countries exhibit few reading problems. In France, with state supported preschools, reading is taught at age three, and 30 percent of French children have reading problems. A recent comprehensive book on reading, called *Proust and the Squid: The Story and Science of the Reading Brain*, relates it to brain development as well as experience—and comes to the same conclusions.

Despite the research, there are those who insist that parents can teach their infants to read, if they will only buy the magical system being offered. One of the first to make this kind of offer was Glenn Doman, with *How to Teach Your Baby to Read*. He argued that because the brain is growing rapidly during the first years, this is the time to teach reading and math. (This claim always puzzles me. As a gardener, one of the first rules I learned was never to prune during the growing season). Although Doman (and now his daughter Janet) have been selling the program for more than forty years, they have no follow-up studies to demonstrate its effectiveness. Others—such as Krista Guerrero, who created MonkiSee—are on the same bandwagon. Guerrero makes similar bogus claims, such as, on the MonkiSee website: "Your baby can actually learn to read beginning at 3 months of age." People who sell these materials offer no research or other evidence in support of their arguments. These purveyors build on parent anxieties in order to sell a product that is likely to do more harm than good.

Reading with comprehension is a very complex skill that requires experience and maturation. It can't be hurried. The best way to prepare your child for learning to learn to read is to provide a language-rich environment by reading, talking, and singing to your child.

Religious Development

I recently received e-mail from a minister who took me to task for something I had written many years ago, in an article called "Age Changes in the Meaning of Religious Identity." The statement in question was based upon some of my early research on children's conceptions of their religious identity. For this study, I interviewed several hundred four- to twelve-year-old Catholic, Protestant, and Jewish children. I posed unusual questions so as to provoke their own ideas, rather than something they might have learned in their religious instruction. One of the questions, for example, was "Can a dog or a cat be a Catholic, Protestant, or Jew?" Another question was "How can you tell a person is a Catholic, a Protestant, or a Jew?"

What I found was that children's conceptions of their religious denomination developed in a series of stages that were related to age and to the stages of intellectual development described by Jean Piaget in *The Psychology of Intelligence*.

Young children, up to the age of five or six, had a *global* conception of their religious denomination and thought of it as general category, such as nationality. When I asked one young child if his dog could be a Protestant he replied, "No he's a black lab." At the second stage, children had a *concrete* sense of their denomination. When asked if his dog could be a Protestant, a seven-year-old said, "Yes, he's part of the family, but no, he'd bark in church and the minister would kick him out." Pre-teens, ages eleven to twelve, had a more *abstract* conception of denomination as a belief system. One twelve-year-old said his dog couldn't be a Protestant because "He isn't intelligent enough and can't understand the Bible."

On the basis of these findings, I made some recommendations with respect to religious education. For example, in my work with adolescents, I found that once they attained the mental abilities that appeared along with puberty, they were able for the first time to appreciate the privacy of their own thoughts. As a consequence, many young teenagers create a personal religion in which God is a confidant who will not reveal the thoughts they have shared with their personal deity. My suggestion for this age group was that religious instruction ought to be put on hold for early adolescents and that the time be used for the discussion of personal and social issues.

It was this suggestion with which the minister took issue. He insisted that religious instruction be maintained to ensure the young person's continuous commitment to his or her religious community. I disagree and believe most young people will come back to the faith of their family with renewed commitment and enthusiasm if given a break from what is all too often tedious religious instruction. I wrote back and said, "Let's agree to disagree."

Responsibility, Teaching

After one of my talks to parents of young children, a mother asked about when she should start teaching her toddler responsibility. My answer was a little long-winded—really unusual of me, of course—but I'll give you the gist of it. I believe that almost from birth parents and children begin to negotiate parent-child contracts. These are, of course, implicit and nonverbal. They are communicated through our interactions.

One of these contracts is what I call the "freedom/responsibility contract." As parents, we reward our children for demonstrating responsibility and withhold rewards when they fail to do what they are capable of doing. Obviously, these contracts have to be rewritten as the child matures and is more capable of taking on more responsibility.

To illustrate, suppose a toddler, for whatever reason, insists on tearing pages out of the books he or she is looking at. After several reminders that books are for reading and not for tearing, we remove the books so that the child no longer has access to them. Because the toddler did not act responsibly when he or she was perfectly capable of doing so, the child loses the corresponding freedom. In the same way, suppose the toddler chooses to mark up the walls, and not the coloring book, with crayons. Again after several reminders that walls are to keep things quiet, not for coloring, the child loses the freedom to use the crayons. What is so important, and where some parents out of the goodness of their hearts make a mistake, is in follow-through—actually taking away the freedom. If you follow through on the freedom/responsibility contract, children get the idea.

As children get older, the contracts are rewritten. Suppose a first grader is told that if he or she puts away his or her toys, he or she can watch a particular television program. Again, it is important to make it clear that the child's toys are not furniture and that they must be put away when he or she is not using them. If the child puts away the toys, he or she gets to watch the program; but if the child refuses, he or she does not get to watch the program. In this way, the child learns that freedom is never absolute and is always dependent upon a demonstration of responsibility. If we are consistent in this practice, by the time a young person is an adolescent, he or she will have internalized the contract. The teen will understand, for example, that if he or she does not come home at a designated time, that the freedom to stay out late again will be restricted.

To some parents, this may seem a little hard-hearted. Yet the adult world works along the lines of the same contract. We are free to the extent that we obey the laws set by our society. Teaching children the freedom/responsibility contract teaches them self-discipline and thus prepares them for responsible citizenship.

Routines

Babies, no less than adults, are creatures of habit. There are so many unexpected and surprising events in life that it is comforting and reassuring to have some happenings that are predictable. This is particularly true for the baby, who has arrived in an utterly foreign world and whose earliest mental ability is to understand and appreciate regularly occurring events. Time is less important than sequence, because it is sequence rather than time which babies can understand and appreciate. But there is no one-size-fits-all routine for babies.

The first few weeks are pretty hectic as the baby begins life outside the womb. After several weeks, more often than not, the emerging routine will go something like this: wake, feed, play, sleep. These activities, and the time between them, will vary from day to day, while the sequence remains the same. Of course you can introduce other activities such as bathing and going out in the stroller into the routine. By about four months, most babies will be with the schedule. For those babies who have still not bought into the pattern, a more clock-oriented schedule can be introduced at this age, to help the baby fall into the pattern.

The important point about routines is not to be too bound by them and to be flexible. If the baby is hungry at 10:00 and isn't usually fed till 12:00, the baby's needs should come first. In addition, a baby's temperament has to be factored into the equation. Some babies feel very comforted by routine and are disturbed by breaks in the pattern. These babies may need a more clock-oriented scheme than babies who deal comfortably with variations in the daily pattern. It is not only the baby's temperament that needs to be taken into account—so does your own. If you are an orderly person and your baby is too, that is a perfect fit. But it doesn't always happen that way. When there is a conflict in this regard, it is important not to blame yourself or the baby, but to recognize that it is simply a difference in temperament. Since it is possible for you, and not for your baby, to understand and adapt to the difference, that is the wisest, if not the easiest, solution.

Life is never as regular as we would like it to be, and it is always presenting us with unexpected challenges. A baby or a parent can get sick, accidents and natural disasters can throw routines into a shambles. We have to recognize that this will happen, deal with the situation, and return to the established routine as soon as possible. Helping the baby deal with variations and breaks in the routine is as important as is setting the routine up in the first place.

S

Sand Play, The Lessons Of

While watching my grand-nieces Raven (three) and Stella Blue (five) one summer, I was again impressed by the freedom, involvement, and concentration of young children's beach play. They dug holes in the sand and enjoyed simply flinging it with their shovels; they filled pails with sand and built a sand castle, then filled the pails with water and washed it away. Stella Blue wanted me to bury her in the sand and seemed delighted as I poured buckets of sand on her feet. She kept urging me to cover her toes as well. These two young children happily occupied themselves for hours on the warm beach sand. This kind of play is easy to understand, but has a larger lesson as well.

When children are at home, at school, or at a public place such as restaurant, they are always being told by adults to follow the rules. At home, they have to pick up what they drop, be sure and not soil their clothes, be careful with their toys, and be watchful about not breaking any household furnishings. At the beach they are free; at the beach it is okay to get dirty and covered with sand (you can just run in the water and wash it off!); you can build sandcastles and destroy them, and no one really cares.

The beach is a place where children are unfettered from the rules that heretofore seemed God-given and unbreakable. They learn that rules are not absolute and that it is okay to get dirty and messy in some places and in some situations. In many ways, the beach is the child's own world, and they cherish having a place of their own, where they can break the adult rules and set their own. It is for the same reason that older children love to build, and to inhabit, tree houses and forts.

Children's beach play has a lesson for parents as well. Such play reminds us that children are smaller and weaker than we are, and that they are dependent upon us for food, clothing, protection, and care. No one likes to be dependent, and this is as true for children as it is for adults. While it is necessary for us as grown-ups to set limits and to socialize our children into the adult world, we also need to find opportunities, such as beach play, for them to be independent and to express themselves in their own way. Such play, in which they create their own rules and are unrestrained by adult conventions, gives them the understanding and confidence that one day they, too, will have control over their own destinies.

School Readiness

In the course of my workshops with teachers, the issue of school readiness for preschoolers comes up often. I have heard many horror stories about children who were held back or even taken out of programs for which they were not "ready." The point I have tried to make to both teachers and parents is simply put:

Readiness is not in the child's head. Readiness is a relationship not a trait. "Readiness" always refers to the relation between the child and the demands and/or the expectations that are being made of or imposed upon him or her. A child, for example, might well be ready for one teacher and one classroom but not for a different teacher and a different classroom.

The problem with viewing readiness as a personal trait, rather than as a relationship, is that it puts the entire onus on the child. If we demand, for example, that every child entering a first grade class knows his or her numbers, then a child who does not have those skills will not be ready for that class. But it is the demands and expectations that are determining the child's lack of readiness, not the child. As I have written in many other places, children grow at very different rates, and this is particularly true in early childhood. To demand that all children be at the same developmental or achievement level because they are the same age is simply a denial of our biological and environmental variability.

In this regard, I recently received an e-mail from a former student who is an early childhood educator. She wrote that she first taught in university lab schools and then returned to college to earn a social work degree. She is now a social worker in birth-to-five programs, and so she attends a lot of parent-teacher meetings. At these meeting she hears parents complain about their child being thrown out of kindergarten because he or she is in need of "improvement." This is a euphemism for a situation where the child can name, say, fifteen rather than the required seventeen letters, or that he or she cannot name ten numbers between ten and twenty. She wrote to me to ask if there were any groups or organizations that were working against this craziness.

I wrote back and told her that as far as I know there is no organized opposition to this madness. Across the United States, in large communities as well as small, as many as 30 percent of children are retained in kindergarten because they do not know their numbers and letters. In effect, these children have failed kindergarten. What a way to start your academic career! Part of the problem is that the first grade has been transformed. When fewer than 50 percent of children were in some type of out-of-home program, first grade curricula had to be flexible to accommodate children with a range of preparation.

Today, however, some 80 percent of children in the US attend some out-of-home program full- or part-time. As a result, first grade has become fully academic and not designed for children who may not know all their letters and numbers.

The irony, as any first grade teacher will fully admit, is that knowing one's numbers and letters is not what a child needs to succeed in first grade. To be successful, a child needs to have attained three social skills.

1. The child must be able to listen to and follow instructions.
2. The child must be able to concentrate and bring a task to completion on his or her own.
3. The child must be able to work cooperatively with other children—stand in line, take turns, etc.

If a child has these skills, the numbers and letters will come easily.

The demand that all children entering first grade must know their numbers and letters rests on several false assumptions. The first is that all early childhood programs emphasize numbers and letters. They don't, particularly the good ones. The second false assumption is that all children progress intellectually at the same rate. But early childhood is much like early adolescence—some adolescents reach puberty at eleven, some at twelve, some at thirteen or fourteen, or even later. They all get there, but they get there at different rates.

The same is true for young children attaining the new mental abilities that the ancients called the "age of reason"—the ability to learn rules and engage in formal education. Some children attain these at four, others at five, others at six or seven. To demand that all children entering first grade know their numbers and letters is equivalent to demanding that all students attain puberty before they enter seventh grade. Making such demands on young children not only makes no sense, it can cause harm. A child's first experiences in school color all of his or her attitudes not only toward school but toward teachers and learning.

We always wait too long in our personal lives and in our social policies. I sincerely hope that we don't wait until we have damaged so many children that we are forced to change a failed policy.

School Refusal

School refusal, formerly called "school phobia," is found in about 5 percent of children and is most common in five-to-six- and ten-to-eleven-year-old children. It usually takes the form of refusing to prepare for school and having violent tantrums and anxiety attacks at the sight of school. School refusal is most often seen when children are undergoing major transitions in their lives, such as entering public school kindergarten, first grade, or junior high or middle school.

When I was a practicing child psychologist, this was one of the most frequent problems brought to our clinic. Fortunately, it is one of the easiest problems to treat and remediate. One of the children I treated presented a fairly typical pattern of this syndrome. Her parents brought her to the clinic because of her resistance to entering public school first grade after attending a private kindergarten. Her parents told me that Dorothy (not her real name) became terrified as she approached the school, threw tantrums, and vomited. Her parents brought her to the clinic because they were at a loss as to what to do.

Her parents were an older couple and after talking with them for an hour, it was clear to me that this was a classic case of school refusal. The parents had inadvertently given their daughter the impression that she was indispensable for their well-being. Her refusal was really an anxiety attack prompted by her separation from her parents and her fear about what would happen when she was not at home to protect them.

The first step in treating such children is to get them into school so the pattern is not reinforced. I encouraged the mother to accompany Dorothy to school and stay with her for the first few days. In the meantime, I helped the parents to communicate to their daughter that they would be fine while she was at school. Reassured in this way, Dorothy was able to go to school on her own.

Although school refusal is most often of the variety described above, it can have other causes as well. Moving to a new city or state, the death of a pet or of someone close, or a divorce can also set off an anxiety attack that can appear as school refusal but is actually a fear of separation. Most children really want to go to school, despite their claims and protests to the contrary. Once parents are helped to appreciate this, and are given tools to alleviate the child's separation stress, school refusal often disappears. It can re-emerge at later ages, though.

My wife and I spent a year in Geneva while I studied with Jean Piaget. To keep up my clinical skills, I volunteered to work as a counselor for the American Church in Geneva, which served American families there. The minister of the church and his family were deciding whether or not to move back to the States after ten years in Switzerland, and he approached me about a problem they were having with their thirteen-year-old daughter. When they began talking about returning to the US, their daughter began having anxiety attacks before going to school. The thought of leaving Switzerland and her friends, and moving to what to her would be a new country, produced the refusal behavior. I encouraged her parents to reassure her that she could come back and visit her friends and have them come visit her. This prompted a number of excited discussions with her friends and helped her deal more comfortably with the move.

School refusal is a fairly common problem. The major things to be done are to get the child to school as quickly as possible and to work with the parents to allay the child's separation anxieties. If handled properly, school refusal is a very easily remediated problem.

Scouting

A while back, I happened to listen to an NPR report on a court case against a scoutmaster in the Northwest. He was being tried for the sexual abuse of some of the boys in his troop. The author of a book on this problem was on the program along with another man, who had devoted his life to scouting. Both men agreed on the value of scouting and that stronger measures should be taken to ensure that those who take on the responsibility of leading a Boy Scout troop be properly vetted. They were not sure how the case would affect enrollment, that is already down considerably from what it had been in the past.

That is too bad. My sons were scouts and got a great deal out of the experience. As a young man, I, myself, was an assistant scoutmaster to an explorer troop. The boys in the troop, often without fathers, profited from working with adult males who could provide positive and supportive role models. It is unfortunate that a few bad apples (even one is too many) can spoil the barrel. But most of the scoutmasters are caring, dedicated individuals and should not be judged by the few who at the very least are not worthy to wear the uniform.

To give some idea of the scope of the Boy Scout organization, consider the following figures from the Boy Scouts of America 2009 annual report: The program had 1 million volunteers and 12,719 local community organizations. It served 1,665,635 boys aged seven to ten years in Cub Scouts, and 905,879 boys aged eleven to seventeen in Explorer Scouts.

Concern about gay scoutmasters is a very different matter from concern about scoutmasters who might engage in sexual abuse. The fear with gay scoutmasters is that they will recruit boys and young men into a "gay lifestyle." An earlier entry has already pointed out that homosexuality is largely genetically determined. Fortunately, such fears are beginning to lessen, as we become more accepting of homosexuality and appreciate that gay men can be effective scout leaders, just as they can be effective soldiers, without their sexual orientation being a threat to others. I believe that boys and adolescents should not be denied effective dedicated leadership, whatever the leaders' sexual orientation.

Second Languages, Learning

For several years I was on the advisory board for the Los Angeles Universal Preschool Project (LAUP), which now serves over ten thousand four-year-olds in the Los Angeles area. The program funds preschool attendance for these children in a variety of preschool and home care centers in the area. They also provide in-service training and coaching for teachers as well as a library of curriculum materials. The advisory board serves mainly to help with the assessment of student progress.

One of the main questions we were trying to answer had to do with second language learning. Close to 70 percent of the children served are non-native speakers of English, and a majority of these children come from homes in which the parents speak Spanish. One of the main questions we were trying to answer has to do with the different approaches to second language learning. Answering the question is complicated because very much depends upon the age of the child and his or her native language proficiency and other factors.

There is a broad range of approaches. At one extreme is what has been called "total immersion," in which the child is instructed only in English and not allowed to use their native language. At the other extreme the "transitional" approach, which allows the child to learn to read in his or her native language before, or while, working on learning English. Even though California passed a law supporting the total immersion approach, the ambiguity of the law allows considerable leeway, particularly at the early childhood level.

Unfortunately, research has not consistently supported either approach. In the LAUP programs for example, the effectiveness of the transition approach depended in part on the language proficiency of the teacher, the amount of time spent using the second language, the language proficiency of the child entering the program, and so on. A large number of studies both in the United States and in Canada have also come up with mixed results.

Nonetheless, there are some general, but far from hard and fast, conclusions. For older children who are already proficient in both speaking and reading their native language, a total immersion program seems to work better than a transitional approach. For young children, however, a transitional program seems to work better than total immersion. It seems that if a child becomes proficient in reading his or her native language, this facilitates learning to read in the second language.

It is certainly true that young children find it easy to learn to understand, and to speak, a second language. But learning to read and to write in a second language is a very different matter. Many people who understand and speak a foreign language may not be able to read or write in that language. I believe that is where the confusion about second language learning comes in. It is easy to assume that because a young child can learn to communicate verbally in two languages, it is equally easy for him or her to learn to read and write in two languages. Not true. Reading and writing are visual and motor skills, while learning to understand and speak a foreign language are auditory and vocal skills. They are not comparable, and reading and writing skills are much more difficult to acquire. That is why reading and writing skills are best learned in one language at a time.

The problem is that schools are not always equipped to provide the kind of second language learning that is most appropriate for children who are non-native speakers. At the very least, teachers of a second language should be fluent in that language if they are to provide good model for children to follow.

Security Blankets

My granddaughter Heather became attached to a cloth bear, which she called "Bear-Bear," when she was two years old. Bear-Bear went with her everywhere, including a visit to us on Cape Cod. Unfortunately, she left Bear-Bear unguarded in a place where our dog, Remy, could get to it. I guess he became attached to it as well, because he bit off one of its ears. We thought Heather would be devastated, but she was relieved when my wife offered to sew the ear back on, which she did. Some damage had been done, and the ear went on at a rakish angle, but Heather was happy and that is all that mattered. She is five now, and she gave up Bear-Bear before her last visit. She did so on her own when she was ready to carry on without him.

There are several theories as to why it is so common for young children to attach to warm cuddly things, which they may cling to for years. One older theory was that children who are poorly attached to their mothers used the cuddly doll or blanket as a substitute. A number of years ago Robert Passman did a study to test the theory, which was reported in "Attachments to Inanimate Objects: Are children Who Have Security Blankets Insecure?" He found no support for this explanation. Indeed, he found no relationship between the strength of the mother-child bond and the child's passion for the doll or blanket. What he did find was that children who were insecurely attached to their mothers but securely attached to their doll or blanket seemed to adjust better to an anxiety-producing (mother absent) situation than did children who were securely attached to their mothers. For the latter children, the presence of the security object promoted play, exploration, and non-distress

A theory that may well help to explain these results was offered by famed English pediatrician and psychiatrist Donald Winnicott. In "Transitional Objects and Transitional Phenomena: A Study of the First 'Not Me,'" Winnicott argued that the security doll or blanket serves as a means of dealing with the infant's separation from the mother. In effect, it served as a substitute or, as Winnicott labeled it, a "transitional object." Transitional objects give the child the time to build up the necessary intellectual and emotional tools for coping successfully with the separation. After that restorative work is done, the child will give up the transitional object on his or her own. Transitional objects are used at later times in life as well. After a divorce or break-up of a long-term relationship, for example, many adults, most often men, immediately find another relationship—a transitional object, if you will—regardless of whether it fits their personalities well.

From this perspective—and this is supported by the research reported above—the security blanket is a healthy way of dealing with a very painful life experience. Because children will give up their transitional objects on their own when they are sufficiently mature, there is no justification for taking them away, and every good reason for allowing each child to give theirs up on his or her own.

Self-Esteem

Reading advertisements for infant stimulation products that promise to raise a baby's self-esteem always angers me. Infants don't really have a self to esteem. The self is a mental construction, which is built up in the course of maturation and does not reach completion, with the attainment of a sense of personal identity, until adolescence. Thereafter, the self continues to be reconstructed in response to life circumstance and aging.

Sociologist George Herbert Mead argued that the self is constructed out of the "reflected appraisal of others." He called it a "looking glasses self." That is to say, our sense of self is, in part, at least, the result of how others respond to us. Even the infant, who does not clearly distinguish between self and others, has an intuitive sense of self. This intuitive self derives in part from the "cuteness factor," nature's way of ensuring that adults smile at infants and young children. These smiles, and other positive reactions, give the infant a sense of acceptance and well-being, a sense of trust that the world is a safe place where his or her needs will be met.

It is only when the child acquires language and begins to use the pronouns "I" and "me" that the self begins to be constructed in a more conscious way. But this new verbal self builds upon the intuitive self that came before it. That is why it is so important to cuddle, smile, and talk sweetly to the infant. And none of that comes from infant stimulation programs. It is important to emphasize that distinguishing between self and the world is an ongoing process. For example, when one of my sons was four, he told me that he had a toothache. I asked him if it was really hurting and he replied, "Yes, can't you feel it?"

It should be said that "self-esteem" is often misunderstood to mean "feeling good about yourself." With this idea in mind, some parents go to great lengths to avoid giving the child any bad feelings. To be sure, we should avoid making a child feel bad for no reason. But we are all human; we make mistakes, say the wrong thing, do the bad thing and hurt others in the process. When a child does something of the kind, it is important to say something like, "That was not a nice thing to do or to say, and it made me feel bad." Guilt is a healthy emotion that can help us to be more thoughtful in our social interactions.

In the end, the most important contributor to self-esteem is the feeling of security, of being very important to another person who cares deeply about you. With that feeling of security, the child is able to cope with much that life has to offer. Without it, the child is vulnerable to all of life's vicissitudes. So real self-esteem can never by learned from infant stimulation programs—it can come only from the commitment and nurturing of loving parents.

Sesame Street

On November 10, 2009, *Sesame Street* celebrated its fortieth anniversary. It was one of the first television programs for children that had educational aims. Indeed, its original intended audience was disadvantaged children. It was initiated as part of Lyndon Johnson's "War on Poverty" and the effort to find ways to raise the educational level of children who were traditionally doing poorly in school. The set for early *Sesame Street* episodes reproduced an inner-city neighborhood street with a grimy but magical look. In keeping with this theme, the Fix-It Shop was a cluttered mess with ailing toasters in the window.

Although the primary aim of the show was to help inner-city children succeed academically, it also tried to teach moral lessons and to bring children to understand that learning can be fun. But from our present perspective, some of the characters and episodes were far from being politically correct. Cookie Monster, for example, was always thinking about food, ate just about everything in sight, and sometimes ate things that would not be in sight today, like a typewriter. Today, thanks to our concern about childhood obesity and the bad example Cookie Monster might provide, he now chooses to eat a more nutritious diet and recognizes that cookies are a "sometimes" food.

Over time, the characters have been softened and the sets have been cleaned up; there are no more garbage cans or sketches in which a real man, not a puppet, invites a girl into his house for milk and cookies. While these changes make sense in terms of today's climate, they also take away from some of the charm of the older shows. I always thought that the older shows were too fast-paced for younger children, for whom *Mr. Rogers' Neighborhood* provided a more welcoming, and less frenetic, fantasy world. Today's *Sesame Street* is slower paced and a little less busy than in the past.

Research has shown that middle-income children who watch *Sesame Street* do better academically, compared with children who watch more action shows like *Spider Man* and *SpongeBob SquarePants* among many others. Yet it is not clear that *Sesame Street* has had the same effect with its target audience, inner-city children. Today, *Sesame Street* has to compete with many other programs and DVDs and apps targeted to children. It nonetheless continues the laudable practice of ensuring that the material is developmentally appropriate. Thanks to the writers, with the collaboration of psychologists and educators, the show remains very thoughtful about the messages it sends to children. In that regard, it remains one of the best of the current programs for young people.

Sex Education

When our first son was still an infant, we visited a psychiatrist friend and his wife who had a three-year-old daughter. The psychiatrist was a Freudian, and very much concerned that children from an early age know the names of all parts of the human body and their functions. It became necessary to change the baby (it was my wife's turn), and the young girl asked if she could watch while this was done in another room. When my wife brought our son back to the living room, the three-year-old returned with her. Without preamble, she announced, quite loudly and proudly, "My daddy's is bigger than his!"

Her comment was funny but we all tried not to laugh and give her the impression that such remarks were appropriate and amusing. And it raised the question of what is appropriate to teach young children about body parts and body functions. This is not really sex education, because young children have no conception of intercourse. Young children and/or their parents often use euphemisms for the penis and for bowel movements. That does no harm, and children will learn the real names for these soon enough.

What is important for young children, indeed for children at all age levels, is health education. Such education involves personal hygiene, diet, exercise, and clothing.

Several years ago, a number of studies in *Pediatric Medicine* reported that sexual abstinence education had little or no effect on the numbers of adolescents who are sexually active or on the number who contract venereal disease. This is no great surprise. I have always been amused by the idea of sex education as a course of study. If "sexual education" were a course of study, we should also have sex education 101, sex education for phys ed majors, sex ed for psych majors, advanced sex ed, and graduate seminar sex ed. Maybe we should grant bachelor's and master's degrees in sex ed. Indeed, there may be a potential Ph.D. program in sex ed.

The point is that sex education was introduced not as a course of study but rather as a means of regulating adolescent sexual behavior. Anyone who has been anywhere near teenagers knows that the last thing that is going to control their behavior is information. Knowledge about the negative effects of smoking, for example, hasn't stopped teenagers who want to smoke from smoking. And sex education is not going to stop those teenagers who want to have sex from having sex. The aforementioned study on abstinence education is simply yet another example of this truth.

In many ways, sex education repeats the mistakes of character education. No curriculum is going to teach a child not to cheat, steal, or lie. We learn the most important lessons of character, as we do of sexual behavior, from the significant people in our lives. Parents who are honest, open, and law-abiding are usually going to have children who are the same. Likewise, parents who regard sexual activity as a normal, healthy, and rewarding part of life are going to convey this to their children. These parents will help young people to understand that sexual activity is a human activity and that it requires thoughtfulness and consideration of the other person. All too many parents, however, feel embarrassed about talking about sex with their children. As a result, most sex education often comes from peers and is often wrong.

So there is a place for sex education in our schools, but it should be part of an overall K–12 health education program. It should not be singled out as something apart from age-appropriate discussions of the body, diet, exercise, and disease. Such a comprehensive health education curriculum is particularly necessary in an age when bad nutrition and recreational sex are often the norm on television, in movies, and in video games. While comprehensive health education is important, it is still the parents' modeling of healthy living habits, and health attitudes toward sexuality, that will have the most impact.

It would be ideal if our behavior were controlled by knowledge and reason, but it is not. Consider that the global spread of education has been matched by the global increase in the number of people killed in wars and by the power of our weaponry. Education is valuable and important, but it is not always what guides human behavior.

Sexualized Too Soon

In an interview before Halloween a few years ago, Diane E. Levin, co-author of the book *So Sexy So Soon,* made the point that costumes for seven- to eight-year-old girls are sexually suggestive—in some cases even looking like the clothing of child prostitutes. Levin suggests this is but a symptom of an ongoing trend to sexualize young girls. The Disney princesses, Miley Cyrus, and Britney Spears provide highly sexually costumes and behavior. For boys, the costumes are macho—G.I. Joe, Transformers, Teenage Mutant Ninja Turtles, and Power Rangers.

These costumes reflect how children are beginning to define their sexual identities and the way they are seen by the opposite sex. When boys look at girls dressed in sexy costumes, they are likely to think that is how girls are supposed to be pretty, and that is the most important thing about girls. For boys, the image is of male toughness, and girls tend to regard boys in this narrow way as well. Levin comments that this way of presenting the sexes to one another is dehumanizing, and does not encourage respect and consideration for a person of the opposite sex.

In *So Sexy So Soon: The New Sexualized Childhood and What Parents Can Do to Protect Their Kids* Levin and Jean Kilbourne provide abundant evidence to support their argument that young children are learning sexual behavior—sexualization—before they understand true sexuality and sexual relationships. This leads to distorted attitudes toward both themselves and the opposite sex, and can have long-term consequences for later healthy sexual adjustment. The closing of a preschool in California because the children were engaging in oral sex is a case in point.

Levin and Kilbourne offer parents many helpful suggestions and strategies for minimizing the damage to their children from too-early sexualization. It does not take away from the value and usefulness of their book to point out that there is another contributor to early sexualization, over and above the media. More of our young children are in child care than ever before. More than 80 percent of our young children are in non-parental care part- or full-time. What this means is that children are being socialized to age-mates earlier than ever before. Even with two-year-olds, one can already observe patterns of social hierarchy, leadership, and followership in a child care center.

As a consequence, children are being introduced to peer pressure, and the need to conform and compete, at earlier and earlier ages. Even four-year-olds now show concern over the logos on their sneakers, jeans, and shirts. This preschool peer socialization appears in other ways as well. Many of the behaviors we once saw among older children, such as relationship bullying (social exclusion), are now appearing at ever-earlier ages.

While some types of early socialization can have strong benefits for cooperative learning, that does not seem to be the way this development is moving. In any case, I think we have to appreciate that it is the early socialization of so many of our contemporary young children that makes them particularly susceptible to media exploitation. Even young children now feel that they have to idolize and imitate the current teen stars or Disney characters in order to be accepted by their peers.

Sharing

During a family visit, I heard my three-year-old grandniece Raven, cry out, "It's mine, and it's mine!" Her older sister was teasing her by trying to put on one of a pair of slippers that had been given to Raven as a Christmas gift. Her sister, still teasing her, said, "You have to learn to share, Raven." What Raven's sister, Stella Blue, did not appreciate, was how difficult a concept "sharing" is for a young child.

For the preschool child, the boundaries of self and world are still fluid, and we need to respect the young child's investment in his or her possessions. When a young child is given a toy or an article of clothing, it becomes part of the self. The young child is unwilling to share not because of selfishness but out of fear of losing part of the self. This is not a phenomenon unique to preschoolers. I have a friend who won't let anyone get near his sports car, much less drive it. And we probably all have certain possessions that we treasure and regard as part of ourselves. The only difference is that preschoolers regard all of their possessions as part of the self.

I know that sharing is one of the social skills that young children are supposed to learn. And there are ways of teaching sharing that take into account the young child's fragile sense of self. For example, suppose at a birthday party Tony wants to play with Sarah's truck. Sarah is unwilling to let him, for the reasons I have outlined above. But suppose you say to Sarah, "Sarah, I am going to make little sign with your name on it and tie it with a little string to your truck." You then make the sign, which might say, "Sarah's truck," read the sign to both children, and then attach it to the truck. Once this is done, you might announce to all the children around, "See, this is Sarah's truck—the sign says so. Now, Sarah, can Tony play with your truck?" Under these circumstances, with the identity of the truck clearly established, Sarah may be more willing to share.

While I fully understand the desire to teach children to share, they may need to learn the opposite as well. With my own sons, for example, I often found that I had to teach them not to let others use their things. One of my son Bobby's friends was always borrowing his things and returning them dirty, bent, or broken. I finally had to say to him, "Bobby, you can't lend Ralph any more of your toys. You know he always destroys them." Sharing, like other social graces, has its limits.

Sibling Rivalry

Our granddaughter Heather just turned five, and she has a new baby sister, Nyla. Heather could not be happier. She loves to be around the baby and is always kissing her when she gets the chance. Her parents allow her to help care for Nyla in ways that are age-appropriate—for example, she brings the new diaper to a parent when this is needed. But of course there will be dark times, when not all is sweetness and light. Nyla will grow older, becoming verbal and mobile, and conflicts are inevitable.

At some point, Nyla, uninvited, will get into Heather's toys, books, clothes, or jewelry. Later, she may want to tag along with Heather and her friends, even though she will be too little to really play their games. So some conflict between siblings is quite normal and to be expected. At such times, and indeed, at all times of sibling conflict, the basic rule is to be an impartial judge and not take sides. While all sibling conflicts have a surface cause (using one another's things, saying things that are hurtful, etc.) they also always have a deeper rationale.

Whenever siblings fight, the underlying purpose is to test the parents to see whose side they will take. All siblings want to be first among equals, and to believe that their parents love them most of all. As parents, we have to be careful not to be taken in. For example, the younger child may often be the instigator, figuring that the parents will automatically blame the older child. The reverse can also be true. When I was young, my older brother and I shared a bed. My brother wet the bed regularly but got up and put me, still sleeping, on the wet spot. When I found out, after not being allowed to drink anything for hours before bedtime, I hit him over the head with his guitar.

Although conflicts are inevitable, we do have options as to how to handle them. In order to avoid playing favorites, it is important to first hear both sides of the story. Actually, having each child tell his or her story tends to calm things down. If the stories don't mesh, then it has to be a draw. If there has been some damage done, then both have to help repair it. Likewise, for any punishment, like TV or computer deprivation, both children have to have restrictions. While it is hard to be impartial, making one child the pet, or favored one, is just asking for trouble. For some unfavored children, it sets a pattern of always trying to find ways to please the parent, or alternatively, ways to make them angry or miserable.

A useful strategy for dealing with the deeper causes of sibling rivalry is for each parent to take each of their children on a regular outing. This one-on-one event can be out to a meal, out to a movie, for a walk, or for a longer trip to visit relatives. Such outings allow the parent to get to know the child apart from his or her siblings and for the child to have the undivided attention of a parent. In this way, each child has the experience of being the favored one with each parent.

This practice will not eliminate sibling rivalry, but it will diminish it by giving each child the sense of being known as an individual and not just one among other siblings. In any case, the one-on-one outing with each child has benefits regardless of the unique configuration of the family.

Sick Children, Stories For

Our first son had asthma from birth. He was born in Denver, where he received excellent pediatric care from a single pediatrician. We moved to Rochester, New York, when he was six, and we immediately made an appointment with a highly recommended pediatric group. When I took him for his first visit, I was immediately put off by the large-scale office arrangement. We were ushered into a train-like corridor of small waiting rooms, and left there. After awhile, an obviously hurried pediatrician came in, briefly introduced himself to me, and asked my son Paul to open his mouth so the pediatrician could take his temperature.

I was upset by this abrupt treatment and told the doctor that before doing any procedures with my son, he had to introduce himself and explain what he was doing and why. The young doctor was a little taken aback, but I explained that I was a child psychologist and that I had taught pediatricians about child development. He appreciated my concern and did as I asked. We later became friends.

At that time, several decades ago, pediatricians were given very little training in child psychology. This has changed over the years, but the pediatric curriculum is still so packed that there is still not much time given to learning about children's intellectual, social, and emotional development. Initiatives called "child life programs," which provide the kind of support and information sick children need, have now been introduced into many children's hospitals.

At the Floating Hospital for Children at Tufts Medical Center, for example, a set of rooms is set aside for the child life program. In this setting, children with prolonged illness can take classes, play games, and watch television. In the Department of Child Development at Tufts, we train students to work in child life programs. The child life worker not only plays with the children but also gets them accustomed to things like shots and blood pressure readings by using toy instruments. Sometimes, a child life worker will even accompany children to the operating room to reassure them and to let them know what is happening. Child life programs aim to remedy the fact that many doctors and nurses simply do not have the time to sit down and explain illness and wellness procedures to children.

Charlotte Cowan recently introduced an alternative to the child life program. She works at the Massachusetts General Hospital, and one day noticed a group of children with asthma waiting to be treated. They were weary, frightened of the breathing nebulizer they were given, and simply scared of the hospital itself. General hospitals often do not have child life programs. Cowan tried to think of a way to help these children, and she came up with the idea of writing books that would help children with different illnesses. Once her own children were grown, she wrote a series of *Hippo* picture books (a pun on the Hippocratic oath). The stories are about animals that get common infections, how their lives are interrupted, and how everything gets back to normal in a week or so.

Cowan cleverly matches the animal patients to the diseases they contract. Not surprisingly, the giraffe gets a sore throat, while the elephant gets an earache. And her titles latch onto children's funny bones. What child at the toilet-humor level could resist *The Moose with Loose Poops*? The five books she has written so far deal with stomachache, ear ache, fever, cold, and strep throat. Her books have had powerful proponents, and she was even invited to the White House for an event honoring individuals who have had a positive impact on society. And her books have indeed been very beneficial to sick children and to their parents.

At last we are beginning to realize that children really need our help in understanding and coping with their own illness.

Sleep Issues: The First Six Months

Sleep patterns are among the most variable of infant behaviors. Some babies go to sleep easily but don't stay asleep for long.

Other babies have trouble falling asleep but once asleep stay asleep. Still other babies seem not to want to go to sleep or to stay asleep. There are, however, some general developmental trends that hold for most infants. During the first three months, infants seldom sleep for more than four hours at a time. They have little tummies and digest mother's milk fast, so they get hungry after only a few hours.

From three to six months, babies stay awake for longer periods and sleep for longer periods as well; some may sleep as long as five or six hours at a stretch. The increase of the length of wake and sleep times continues during the second half of the first year. By the end of the first year, most infants sleep through the night.

It is important to distinguish between light sleep and deep sleep. You can tell babies are in light sleep when their eyes are shut but their eyelids continue to flutter and their breathing is irregular; their hands and feet are flexed, and they may show restless movements and fleeting smiles. If you put a baby down in their bed at this time, they are likely to awaken and cry. This is because he or she was not fully asleep. It is better to wait, sometimes as long as twenty minutes, until babies are into deep sleep before putting them down. Babies are in deep sleep when their breathing becomes regular, their muscles relax and go limp, and the twitching and smiling stop. It takes babies longer to go into deep sleep, but if you wait until they do before you put them down, they are less likely to awake and cry.

Night waking during the first six months of life is healthy. A baby will waken for several reasons. It appears that brain growth is more rapid during light sleep than deep sleep, perhaps because a child is more active during light sleep. Equally important, the infant's nutritional needs for frequent feeding are a good reason for him or her to wake up. So while the first few months of frequent night waking are hard on parents, they are essential for the baby's healthy development.

Sleep Issues: The Second Six Months

During the second six months of life, babies begin to sleep for longer periods but may still wake up during the night. This may reflect the fact that they are developing, and trying to practice, in their sleep, new skills such as crawling, standing, and coordinating eyes and hands. But it can also be due to the infant's new mental construction of the mother as a permanent object who continues to exist when she is no longer present to the infant's senses. This concept gives rise to the baby's strong attachment to the mother and to stranger and separation anxiety. It can also contribute to the baby's reluctance to go to sleep and his or her waking in the middle of the night. Again, infants vary a good deal in this regard, but waking at night toward the end of the first year is a common occurrence.

By the last quarter of the first year and into the second year, it is not necessary to rush to the baby when he or she cries. At this stage the baby needs to learn to handle a certain amount of stress. By the end of the first year, the infant can tolerate a little bit of anxiety and panic, and it is healthy for him or her to learn to do so. For example, after feeding, if the baby is left alone and fidgets and cries, this will usually die down after a few moments. This is true at bedtime as well. The cries and protests after the bedtime rituals have been gone through will quiet themselves if you do not rush in the moment the baby acts up.

Of course if the baby goes into a real panic, it is necessary to go in and reassure him or her. But it is often enough to speak to the baby in a comforting tone and to pat her softly. It is really not necessary to pick the baby up and hold her and rock her or try to feed her or to entertain her. You don't want to reinforce this soothing behavior by making it so rewarding the baby will do it for the rewards rather than because he or she is upset.

While it may be tempting, particularly if you are exhausted, to take the baby into your bed, this is probably not a good idea, at least for you. From the baby's point of view it is a capital idea, and a good reason for the infant to cry once he or she is put back into his or her own bed. Once they have had the experience of sleeping with you, they can get really upset if you don't let them do it again.

In general, then, as babies get older, they need to learn to tolerate separation and other social stresses. They learn this best if we respond to their distress with some comforting responses. But at this stage, toward the end of the first year, the general rule is that less is more than enough.

Sleep Training Methods

A number of methods have been suggested for training babies to sleep. They all make sense, but there is no one-size-fits-all, so I will describe several that might be tried out.

One sleep training method, now commonly referred to as the "cry it out method," was introduced by pediatrician Richard Ferber in his book *Solve Your Child's Sleep Problems*. The idea is to teach the baby to fall asleep on his or her own by progressively increasing the waiting time before responding to the child's cries. Not surprisingly, this method has often been misunderstood as simply letting the baby cry until he or she goes to sleep. Although this progressive method may work for some infants there are other things to consider.

First and foremost is the infant's age. The world for a newborn is a completely foreign environment; it is like suddenly being dropped onto another planet. The young infant is not fully aware of what is making him or her cry, only that there is something causing discomfort. You cannot spoil a young infant. What the young infant needs to know is that the world is a safe place and that his or her needs will be met. This means picking up the baby and finding out where the discomfort comes from—hunger, wetness, irritation, and so on. The cry-it-out method should be introduced only after the baby feels secure in his or her new world, after the age of four or five months.

The second most important thing to consider is the uniqueness of each child. There is no single best child rearing practice. A number of pediatricians have offered alternatives to the cry-it-out method that speak to the matter of individual differences. Famed pediatrician T. Berry Brazelton, for example, suggests talking soothingly and murmuring, "You can go to sleep, you can do it." Pediatrician Harvey Clark, who suggests modifying the environment to ease the baby into sleep, offers another approach. He suggests that playing white noise, from a fan or special machine, will do the trick.

Jodi A. Mindel suggests a modified Ferber approach and advocates putting the baby to bed while he or she is still alert and then popping in periodically if he or she is crying.

Because no one method works with all babies, it is well to keep all of these methods in reserve and keep trying them until you find the one that works for your baby.

I would like to add one other point that I find missing from these approaches, namely, that nature of the child's cry. Not all crying is the same, and we, as parents, need to learn to tell cries that are just to call us back from cries that signal pain and discomfort. At the same time, it is important that the baby learns to go to sleep on his or her own, so you should use whatever method works. Otherwise, you will be in the position of some parents I have known, who still have to be with the child at bedtime, even during the preschool years.

Learning to go to sleep on one's own is a healthy part of growing up, and we need to use whatever method works to help babies achieve that goal.

Social Exclusion

While visiting our niece and her children recently, I observed a familiar phenomenon. My niece has three children, but there is also an older cousin, Halley, who lives nearby and who is often playing with Stella Blue, the oldest of my niece's three girls. Until the baby, Willow, was born, Raven, now the middle child, was always excluded from the play of Halley and Stella Blue. Her efforts to be included in their play were simply rebuffed. Unfortunately, this has become a habit, and now Halley and Stella Blue mother the new baby and continue to exclude Raven from their games.

Three just happens to be a bad number, sociologically speaking. At Tufts University, where I taught until I retired, we found that three students in a dorm room simply didn't work, and you had to have either two or four to avoid problems and complaints. Many other universities and boarding schools have found the same to be true.

It is also true for families with three children who are born within a few years of one another. Usually, two of the children partner off against the third—not unusually the middle child. The struggle of middle children to find their identity, being neither the oldest nor the youngest, is thus compounded by the rejection of their siblings.

The trouble with three is not just among siblings. School-age children, most often girls, demonstrate the same issue. But with three girlfriends, the ones who are in and the one who is out keeps changing. So there sometimes appears to be a rotating third girl out. A girl who is complaining about one girl one week, will be the complained-about girl's best friend the next.

For boys it is athletic ability and game skills rather than numbers that determines who is in and who is out. And for boys, the exclusion is not as changeable as it is for girls.

As children get older, the process of social exclusion gets extended to groups. Both boys and girls often form clubs, from which some children are excluded. This process of social exclusion has the same purpose among children as it does for adults. Exclusion gives the excluder a sense of superiority over the excluded. Being excluded is hurtful to adults, and it can be very painful to a child, who has not had the time to develop defenses against such rejection.

Fortunately, social rejection from being the odd person out is usually corrected with time. As children grow older they acquire their own friends and no longer worry so much about their relationship to siblings. The same is true for three-girl friendships. By the time they are grown up, most children have overcome any lasting effects of being excluded on the basis of being the excluded third. It must be said, however, that for some children such exclusion can have long-lasting effects upon their personalities.

It is never fun to be excluded, either by your siblings or your peers. As parents, there is not a lot we can do about this other than to reassure the excluded child of his or her many positive qualities and to show him or her a little special care and attention. This can help, in part, at least, to make up for the hurtful behavior of their siblings and/or peers.

Spanking

One of the most controversial issues in child rearing is that of spanking. I have spoken to many parents who tell me that they were spanked as children and that they learned from it and intend to use the same method with their own children. Other parents see spanking as a form of corporal punishment that has a negative effect. Aggression, they believe, begets aggression. Experts disagree as well, with some advocating spanking and others advising strongly against it.

My own position is somewhere in the middle. I must admit that I once did lash out at my sons. I was driving down one of the six-lane Los Angeles freeways and trying to change lanes to get ready to exit. The boys were fighting and carrying on, and I couldn't concentrate and was sure I would get into an accident. Yelling at them did no good, so a reached back and swung my arm at them, probably hurting myself more than them, but they got the message. Sometimes, dire circumstances require dire measures.

In general, though, I don't believe in spanking once children have reached the age of reason—six or seven. For young children, spanking can sometimes serve the useful purpose of instilling healthy fears. If a child tries to run into a busy street, we communicate our fear and anxiety by a healthy smack on a usually well-padded bottom. This should be accompanied with a verbal expression of the danger and our fear and anxiety over their being hurt. When the smack follows closely on the action, it is a learning experience. On the other hand, spanking a child long after an event, particularly by the non-involved parent, makes it hard for the child to put the two things together. That kind of spanking is likely to do more harm than good.

When children are older, we can communicate our anger in ways that do not attack the child's personality or character. We have to restrain our tendency to over-generalize and to say things like, "You are such a slob" or "Can't you do anything right?" It may be a one-time lapse, but such words have life-long effects.

With my own children, I found that expressing my anger with humor allowed me get the feeling out of my system without attacking their personalities, "The next time you do something like that I am going send you to the moon!" "The next time you say something like that I am going to tie your tongue into knots!" Our feelings as parents are appropriate and need to be communicated. But it is best if we can get our message across without character assassination.

In general then, I don't think spanking is an either/or issue. Even with older children, a physical expression of our fear and anxiety may be called for, and usually has no lasting consequences. But corporal punishment should be reserved for rare and compelling circumstances. With young children, a swat on the rear end in circumstances in which we want to instill learned fears—of cars, fire, sharp instruments—serves a useful purpose. Outside of such situations, other tactics, such as distraction, rewards, and withholding rewards get the job done without damaging our relationship with our children.

So spanking, or corporal punishment, should have a place in our disciplinary tool chest. But it should be used only in those circumstances where it is either necessary for the safety of all involved or required to instill healthy fears in young children. In most cases, other disciplinary techniques will be more effective and give our children a model of healthy strategies for when it comes to rearing their own children.

Special Needs Children

Children with special needs pose a huge challenge to parents. How parents cope and how the child turns out depends a great deal upon parental attitude. I have had a number of friends with children with a variety of special needs, ranging from the intellectual to the physical and some combinations of the two. I am always impressed by how well these children do because the parents accepted them as a child who is entitled to everything their other children were given. My wife's aunt and uncle had eight children, one of whom had Down syndrome, but she was given no special privileges and learned to hold her own. When a brother called her "Retard," she came right back at him with "Jug-ears." She is over fifty now and still works every day at a facility created by her father for special needs children.

One of the children of a colleague of mine some years ago had a child of limited intellectual ability. But he was reared in the same manner as his brothers and sisters and was given no special attention other than what was needed when appropriate because of his limitations. He was a great kid—uninhibited, fun to be with, and accepting of his limitations, which he dealt with in adaptive, socially acceptable ways. For example, if he needed help, he would ask for it without embarrassment or hesitation. To the amazement of everyone but his family, he graduated from high school. His parents demonstrated what thoughtful, caring parents could accomplish with a child who has special needs.

At the other extreme are those parents who see having a special needs child as a kind of punishment, bad luck, or just another example of how life has kicked dirt on them. These parents find it hard to accept the child as he or she is, and are constantly trying to deny the reality and to find ways to make the child "normal." Other parents accept the reality of the child but try and hide their child from public view, as if he or she is some sort of a stigma. When the parents behave in this way, the siblings of the child also adopt this attitude and are ashamed to bring friends home. In such families, it does not take superior or even average intelligence for a special needs child to learn how he or she is seen by parents and siblings. Even children of very limited ability soon intuit that they are an unwanted family member at best, and some sort of freak of nature at worst, unfit to live in society.

What I have learned from my friends and my former colleague is that children with special needs test our humanness. For such children give us the opportunity us to discover our deepest humanity, our ability to love and cherish those who are less fortunate. That is perhaps the greatest gift of all.

Sudden Infant Death Syndrome (SIDS)

SIDS is the sudden, unexpected death of an infant under one year of age. According to Boston Children's Hospital, SIDS is sometimes called "crib death" because the death most often occurs when a baby is sleeping in a crib. "The death is sudden and unpredictable; in most cases, the baby is apparently healthy. It occurs quickly, usually when the baby is sleeping. More boys than girls die of SIDS, and the majority of deaths occur between one and four months of age." It is, according to the KidsHealth website, the most common cause of death of babies from one month to one year of age.

About 2,500 babies now die of SIDS each year in the United States. This is half the number that died in 1990. The reduction is due in large measure to an information campaign alerting parents to the major risk factors associated with this syndrome. One of the most dangerous risk factors is for a baby to sleep on its stomach rather than on its back. Smoking during and after pregnancy is also major risk factor: infants whose mothers smoke are three times more likely to die of SIDS than are babies whose mothers do not smoke. Passive smoke from an environment in which there are smokers, even if it is not the mother, is a risk factor as well. Babies whose mothers had little or no prenatal care and were less than twenty years of age when they gave birth are more likely to die of SIDS. Premature and low birth weight babies are also more at risk than full-term infants.

Research on SIDS has been ongoing for more than thirty years, but definitive causes of SIDS have yet to be found. In addition to the risk factors described above, a number of conditions have been found in some, but far from all, or the majority, of SIDS cases. Some infants have brain abnormalities that put them at risk for SIDS; others have immune system problems; still others may have metabolic disorders. But by far the most salient causes are mothers who smoke during pregnancy and putting infants down to sleep on their stomachs. In addition to not smoking and putting the baby to sleep on his or her back, there are other precautions parents can take. The baby should have a firm, not soft, mattress. Blankets and comforters should not be put under the baby. Babies also should be kept warm, but over-heating and over-dressing the baby should be avoided. The temperature in the baby's room should feel comfortable to an adult.

Research has greatly helped to reduce the number deaths from SIDS. This is due to parents who are aware of, and take measures to avoid, the major risk factors (smoking and babies sleeping on their stomachs) that have been identified as associated with SIDS.

Summer Safety

I always know it is springtime when my wife gives me the dates for the annual summer visits of our extended family to our home on Cape Cod. We have a number of infants and young children among our guests, and it reminds us to be prepared for both the pleasures and some of the summer health risks, especially to the very young.

We are on the ocean and do not have a pool. But the ocean presents its own risks. We always have the young children wear a light safety vest whenever they are playing near the water. And we make sure that an adult is always there to watch over them. An errant wave can easily knock a child over. This seems obvious, but after spending many summers on the beach, I have observed too many young children left alone playing in the water.

The sun presents another issue. Infants and young children have very sensitive skin. They really need to be heavily coated with sunscreen. Baby sunscreen of SPF (sun protection factor) 15 or higher is recommended, but I buy the SPF 50 for the kids and use it myself. (There are now some natural sunscreens with fewer chemicals, but I haven't tried them.)

When I put the lotion on the kids, their mothers remind me to put it on all over, including ears and toes. They also tell me to put it under the shorts or tops because these can hike up while the children are playing. The sun is strongest between around 11:00 and 2:00, so it is best to keep young ones out of the sun during those hours. An overheated baby is a grouchy baby. Children can still play in the sand during these hours, but in the shadow of a sand umbrella.

Summer food is another issue. Foods go bad quickly in warm weather, particularly chicken and other cold cuts. Do a smell test and visual check before offering a sandwich of these to a child. An unpleasant odor or shininess is good reason for discarding these items. Parents really have to be careful about this because young children are more sensitive to food contamination than adults are. We also always bring a large cooler down to the beach and include plenty of water. It is easy to get dehydrated in hot weather, and it is important to make sure young children drink a lot of fluids when they are playing in the sun.

Last but not least are the bugs. We have two mosquito traps going all the time, and I usually have to empty them every couple of weeks because they are full. They help a little, but we still can't stay out of doors once the sun starts to set. And there are several weeks of green flies that are on the beach all day long. Insect repellant, preferably the least harsh, should be applied to a baby only after he or she is five or six months old. We also have a lot of ticks in our area, and a tick inspection when the children come indoors is mandatory.

We enjoy the many children who come to visit us during the summer. We take the above precautions to ensure that our young guests really enjoy their visit and that they are eager to return.

Swimming Classes, Infant

I read an article on infant swimming classes the other day, and it reminded me of a book I reviewed several years ago on infants and pools. The author wrote the book in response to a number of cases where infants had drowned after accidentally falling into the family pool. She promised that by using her method, parents could teach their baby to "tread water for up to two hours until help comes."

As I wrote in my review, this is the very worst reason for putting a baby in a swimming class. It is not the infant's responsibility to save himself or herself from drowning. Any family that has a pool and young children should make sure that the fence around the pool is closed when the family is not using it. With a family pool, it is up to the parents to ensure that the pool is child-safe.

It is certainly true that most babies love the water, so swimming classes can be fun for an infant. They can also be a beginning social experience. Swimming classes are provided by the YMCA and by the Red Cross. Most classes take infants six months or older, at which age they can hold their heads up on their own. There is no guarantee that such classes, if not continued during the preschool period, will ensure that the child feels comfortable in the water when he or she gets older. Swimming classes should be looked at as an outing for parents and children and a break from routine, not necessarily as lessons in learning how to swim.

If you are considering taking your baby to a swimming class, there are a number of things to look for. First and foremost, it should be a clean facility with lifeguards and appropriate safety equipment. Second, in the same vein, you should be given instructions on how to dress the baby so that if accidents happen, the water won't be fouled. You should also make sure that the instructor is focused on fun and safety, not swimming skills that the baby is really not capable of learning. Although you will be in the pool with your baby, I still think the instructor should have no more than four parent-baby combinations at a time. Water temperatures should be comfortable, between 86 and 92 degrees.

Although swimming classes can be a fun outing for parents and infants, there are risks. Although babies don't like to put their heads in the water, they can still get splashed, and there is the possibility of middle ear infection. Some infants may be allergic to chlorine and develop skin rashes. But if you and your baby enjoy the outing and you are on the lookout for any negative reactions, it can be a pleasant break from routine.

T

Talking, Late

Many children who talk at a later age then expected are simply "late bloomers," like Albert Einstein, who didn't speak till he was four. Most late talkers usually catch up with their age-mates with a little language enrichment. But for some children, late talking can be a sign of a more serious problem that requires professional attention.

The pattern of language development is well established. Babbling—the infants spontaneous production of the vowel and consonant sounds basic to any language—usually appears around the sixth or seventh month of life. By the end of their first year, most infants have already said their first words. During their second year, most children begin to use a kind of two or three word abbreviated sentence—for example, "Baby up" or "Baby bye." By the end of the third year, most children will speak in short but complete sentences, and know both their name and gender.

A child considered to be a late talker has an active vocabulary (able to speak easily identified words) of less than ten words by the age of eighteen to twenty months. The identification is much more definite if by thirty months of age the child has an active vocabulary of less than fifty words and does not use two or three short-hand sentences. If you suspect that your child has a language delay, it is important to have him or her evaluated by a language specialist. Your pediatrician can recommend one. The usual therapy involves a variety of vocal exercises and practice.

Whether or not your child has a language delay, there are many things you can do to enrich your child's language development. When your child is an infant, it is important to talk, sing, or even recite poetry while you are engaged in routines like eating, changing, or putting to sleep. Toward the end of the first year it is very helpful if you repeatedly name things. Handing your child a fork, you might say "fork," and giving him or her a cup, you might say "cup." Repeating these words along with the objects they represent helps the child to attach words to things and to hear the sounds that he or she will attempt to imitate. Reading to your child, reciting nursery rhymes, and playing games like patty-cake all provide a rich language environment for your child.

A caution: As your child becomes more proficient with language, he or she will of necessity make mistakes. Plurals are particularly difficult when the plural is not made with an *s*. A child who says "feets" indicates that he or she has learned the rule but not the exception. The basic strategy here is to avoid corrections, like saying, "Don't say 'feets,' say 'feet.'" There is an implicit criticism in correction that can inhibit the child's speech. Modeling is a far better approach: "Lets put your shoes on your feet." Modeling gives the child the opportunity to self-correct, which is more rewarding and effective.

The important point is that the majority of late talkers do catch up with a little extra time and language enrichment.

Teaching by Listening

In an article called "Teaching by Listening: The Importance of Adult Child Conversations in Language Development," published in the journal *Pediatrics*, Frederick Zimmerman and his colleagues reported a study in which they interviewed 275 families selected to represent a cross-section of the US population as a whole. The families had children between the ages of two and four. The aim of the study was to assess the effects of adult language input, television viewing, and parent-child conversations on young children's language acquisition. The measures used to assess these three variables were repeated after a year to evaluate their long-term impact on children's language ability.

The results were interesting because they reflect the complexities of the impact of the language environment on children. The adult language input, measured by a count of words used by parents, had a significant positive effect on language acquisition but was more effective when paired with parent-child conversations. Television viewing had a negative effect on language learning, but the negative effect was minimized when combined with parent conversations. Parent-child conversations had the most positive effect, and they enhanced the impact of parent language usage, and reduced the negative effect of television viewing.

Parent-child conversations thus appear to be the most important factor in nourishing a child's linguistic development. For parents, this suggests that while reading to children is very important, two-sided conversations are even more so. Such conversations begin by your really listening to what your child is saying. This can be facilitated if you bend down or kneel to the child's level and tilt your head to indicate that your are really listening. Repeating what your child said is another way to ensure that you have heard correctly. It is important, whenever possible, to respond when a child attempts to initiate a conversation. When you can't, it helps if you say, "I can't talk now because I'm doing something I can't stop. We'll talk in a few minutes, okay?"

Conversations can be of different types. Sometimes, you can put the child's feelings into words when he or she is unable to do so. "You look like you are not happy about going to the babysitter today." Of course you have to use this tactic sparingly and avoid it when the child is very upset. In that circumstance, you might simply aggravate the situation. If the incident involves an interaction with another child, or sibling, it is important for you not to take sides and to ask each child for their version of the event. This often has the added benefit of calming the situation down.

Watching television with your child can often provide openings for conversation. "Was that a kind thing for SpongeBob to do?" In asking questions, it is important keep them simple and direct. Whenever possible, use the child's own words in response to the child's input. Helping children identify and label their feelings is one of the most useful benefits of conversations with children. And the added benefit of such conversations, as this study demonstrated, is to offset some of the negative effects of television viewing on young children.

Television, Young Children And

The evidence for the negative effects of TV watching on infants and toddlers continues to grow. In one study, the investigators looked at a television on in the background affected the quality of interaction between parents and children ("The Impact of Background Television on Parent Child Interaction"). Fifty children between the ages of twelve and thirty-six months participated in the study. Each child and one parent was brought into a lab which was set up to resemble a typical living room. The quality of the parent-child interaction was observed during a half an hour while the television was on—showing an adult program—and for another half hour while the television was off.

Results showed that both the quality and quantity of child-adult interaction decreased in the presence of background television. The study suggests that when the television is on, even if children are not watching it, that it can have a negative effect on the interactions with parents that are so crucial for healthy development.

A closely related study using a very different technology came up with similar results. In this study ("Audible Television and Decreased Adult Words, Infant Vocalizations and Conversational Turns"), children were exposed to audible television, and their vocalizations and those of their parents were recorded by a digital recorder that was sewn into a pocket of the child's clothing. Three hundred and twenty children aged three- to forty-eight-months-old participated in the study. Parents were randomly assigned one day a month to have their child wear the device for a twelve- to sixteen-hour period. The recorders had voice recognition software that has been shown to have high reliability in identifying child, adult, and non-vocal sounds.

Results were very clear. For each hour of audible television to which a child was exposed, there was a significant reduction in child vocalizations, vocalization duration, and in the word count of adult male and female vocalizations. The authors of the study concluded that their results help to explain the now well-established association between television viewing and delayed language development.

Together, these two studies provide more powerful reasons why the television should not be left on all day, as is all too common in many homes. This practice is particularly harmful for infants and toddlers. Infancy and toddlerhood are periods in which a rich human language environment, including talking, reading, and singing to the child, is all-important for healthy overall development. These studies provide a strong argument for limiting a child's television exposure until after he or she is two years or older.

Temper Tantrums

Some of the most troublesome behaviors of young children are temper tantrums, or emotional meltdowns. These are most common during the first three years, but they can happen at later ages, too. The first thing to remember when a very young child is having a meltdown is that at this age children's emotions are not differentiated and the child has little control over them. Anger, fear, and frustration are really not separate, and the child is responding in a global way to a stressful event.

What is most stressful at this age is an experience that somehow frustrates the child's efforts to assert his or her individuality—the reason this age is called *Trotzalter* in German, "the age of pride." If we appreciate that the child is reacting to some threat to his autonomy or sense of self, it helps us to keep our cool, and not see the tantrum as a reflection of our child rearing or an effort by the child to embarrass us.

Of course the best way to deal with tantrums is to try and avoid them. One way is to give young children limited choices— no more than two—in simple language. "Vanilla or chocolate?" "The red shirt or the blue one?" It is also important to appreciate that tantrums often occur when a child is over-tired, hungry, or ready for a nap; many tantrums can be avoided simply by making sure his or her immediate needs are being met.

Of course all tantrums cannot be avoided. Once they are under way, there are a few strategies that might end the meltdown. One of these is distraction. If you are out walking, you might find something interesting to look at, pointing to a dog, a truck, or something else that is different and say, "Oh my goodness! Look at that!" Also, when going on an outing, it is useful to bring along a favorite toy or cuddly animal to bring out as a distracting device in case of a tantrum.

The important thing to remember is that tantrums are normal for young children who are just learning to bring their emotions under control. If we recognize this and don't take the tantrum as directed at us or as a reflection on us, we can deal with it in a calm and considerate way. In so doing we are also providing the child with a model of controlling one's emotions.

If we give in to a child's tantrums and provide them whatever they were angry about not getting, we reinforce bad behavior. In so doing we set the stage for tantrums at a later age—tantrums that are more intentional and manipulative than they were when the child was younger. So perhaps the best way to deal with tantrums is to view them as opportunities to help young children bring their emotions under control.

Temperamental Differences

There is an ongoing debate among psychologists as to which human traits are inborn and which are learned. Over the years, there has been a swing from nature to nurture and back again, in keeping with new research findings. Today, it is generally accepted that it is not an either/or situation: some traits are more inborn than learned while the reverse is true for others.

A number of decades ago pediatricians Alexander Thomas and Stella Chess, and development psychologist Herbert Birch, observed temperamental differences in infants that seemed to persist at least through the early childhood years. Additional research has confirmed the validity of these temperament variations. Because these differences were observed soon after the infants were born, they were assumed to be largely genetic. Nonetheless, as some children grew older, the temperamental differences became more pronounced, while the reverse was true for other children.

Thomas, Chess, and Birch observed three temperamental types, which they described in *Temperament and Behavior Disorders in Children*. First there were the infants whom the researchers labeled "easy to please." Easy children quickly adapted to regular feeding and sleeping schedules and were open to new situations and did not fuss when frustrated. They were generally happy children who smiled a lot.

Another temperamental type they labeled "difficult." These children did not settle easily into regular eating and sleeping patterns. They did not handle new situations well and became upset when frustrated. Socialization seemed to be the big problem for these children, particularly after they began to interact with peers.

The third temperament type was labeled "slow to warm up." These children initially did not adapt easily to eating and sleeping patterns, or to new or frustrating situations. In contrast to the difficult infants, however, the slow-to-warm-up infants eventually adapted to regular routines and could take new situations and frustrations in stride.

Thomas, Chess, and Birch found that about 60 percent of the infants they observed fell into these types, with the remaining 40 percent showing mixed patterns. They also observed how the environment affected temperamental traits. "High-activity" difficult children had problems when they were in a restricted space, were on rigid schedules, and had few outlets for their need for motor activity. "Persistent" slow-to-warm-up children were troubled when an activity they were engaged was prematurely interrupted. "Distractible" difficult children became upset when they were expected to persist too long at a particular activity.

Identifying your baby's temperament is important. Too many parents blame themselves and their child rearing if the child is difficult or slow to warm up. We need to remember that temperamental differences are largely inborn tendencies, not patterns written in stone. Once we appreciate that it is not our fault, we can show the patience and care that can lessen, rather than exaggerate, these initial temperamental variations.

Terrible Twos

We usually think of adolescence as the age period during which young people seek to construct a sense of personal identity, of who and what they are. Yet the search for a sense of personal identity begins much earlier. Indeed, we can see it at the age of two, when children acquire language and the ability to verbally identify themselves.

In order to attain a beginning sense of self, children may use "no" as a way of asserting their will over and against the wishes of their parents. The rebelliousness of the two-year-old is more than simply a way of separating himself or herself from others. It is also an effort at self-control. Often the young child is saying "no" to impulses he or she would like to control.

At this age the child is acquiring bladder control, and is also being told not to engage in certain behaviors, like eating things off the ground. So the young child's nay-saying is both an attempt to define the self in opposition to others and an attempt to define the self over his or her own impulses.

We can handle a two-year-old's negativism most effectively if we don't regard it as a personal attack. It makes little sense to reason with a two-year-old. For one thing, he or she will be unable to follow the argument. More importantly, it is not a rational but an emotional issue, and has to be handled as such.

We need to accept and respect the child's need for self-definition and for self-control. And we have to appreciate that this is a difficult learning effort at which a child may not always succeed. One of the most effective strategies is to verbalize the situation for the child: "I see—Bobby doesn't like peas and carrots. That's okay. Maybe the next time we have them you will feel differently." Or, "I get it Lily—you really don't like this yellow dress. Let's try another." By verbalizing and accepting the child's rejection of food or clothing, we communicate that their effort at self-definition has succeeded. This approach can often nip additional conflict in the bud.

Self-definition with respect to others, and to our own impulses, is a life-long process. We help our children most if we accept and facilitate this process when it first appears in the two-year-old. When we do this, our child learns that self-definition is an ongoing effort and that it is not a disaster if it does not always succeed.

Thoughtless Comments by Adults

Becoming a mother after forty has both blessings and curses—well, not curses maybe, but certainly a lot of thoughtless remarks. Although having a baby after forty is a lot more common than it was in the past, it is still the exception rather than the rule. Mature moms out shopping or dining with their young children are apt to hear remarks like, "Oh, what a beautiful granddaughter you have!" Equally thoughtless is the comment of someone who recognizes that you are the mother and says something like, "Oh, you have a change-of-life baby!" or "Was it an accident or did you really plan it?" or, perhaps most obnoxious and out of line, "How old are you?"

Interestingly, by far the majority of these comments come from women. Men seem to be either totally unaware of these issues or too embarrassed or intimidated to comment. In most cases, it probably makes the most sense to ignore the comment; you will probably never see the person again, so there is little benefit in getting into a discussion about it. If you do feel the need to respond, there are number of options, depending upon the kind of comment being made.

In order to have an appropriate response to such uninvited and inappropriate comments, you need to have some understanding of the motivation behind them. Well-intentioned but ill-thought-out comments about you being the grandmother are probably best dealt with by a polite "Thank you." Most of the other comments arise because something about the idea of a mature women having an infant triggers emotions in other women. For some, it may simply be envy, because of their own repressed wish to have another baby. For others, it may be a kind of emotional lighting rod for resentments against babies and motherhood. For others, it may simply be bird-brained thoughtlessness. Whatever their motivation, such comments are demeaning at best and hostile at worst.

There are several possible lines of response. If the comment really upsets you and makes you angry, you might respond in kind with an equally hostile remark, "I don't know you. It is really none of your business." If you are not much bothered by the remark, you can simply ignore it and say, "My child is just the most joyous gift my husband and I could ever imagine." Last, but certainly not least, if you are feeling particularly happy and thankful for your child, you might respond with humor, "Sometimes, it really pays off to take a romantic vacation with your husband."

People can be cruel, but they can be kind and considerate as well. The remarks of a few thoughtless strangers should not be generalized to all. Nor should they overshadow the many considerate good wishes that also come your way.

Time-Outs

One of most common strategies used by parents for dealing with misbehavior in their children is to put them in a "time-out." This usually involves the child going to his or her room or sitting on a chair in a corner. Presumably, the time-out gives the child time to cool off and to reflect on his or her behavior. Since the time-out is a punishment, the child will realize that to avoid time-outs in the future, the punished behavior is to be avoided.

Yet my friend the late Otto Weininger argued in his book *T.I.P.S.: Time-In Parenting Strategies* contends that time-outs seldom have the desired effects. He argues that children rarely if ever use the time-out to reflect on their misbehavior. Indeed, they may even use the time to plot ways of getting away with the behavior without being caught. Put differently, the time-out is a treatment of symptoms, not causes.

When a child is misbehaving, it is usually out of anger, frustration, fear, or some other emotion. The child most often is not fully aware of where these feelings come from, only that he or she is upset. What children need most at such times, according to Weininger, is a "time-in" with a parent. Children have not fully differentiated their emotions one from the other. They need someone to help them identify and label the feelings that lead to the misbehavior.

In a time-in, parent and child can explore what people or events brought on the feelings. In this way, the child gains both control over his or her emotions and insight as to what brings them on. What the child also learns is that his or her feelings are legitimate, and it is not the feelings but the associated behaviors that are at fault. So the child learns more adaptive ways to express feelings—for example, putting anger into words rather than into actions.

It is certainly true that there are occasions when a time-out may be necessary. If you have several young children and one is acting up so that the others can't be attended to, a time-out may be in order. But on such occasions, it is important to recall Weininger's thoughtful insight, namely, that "time-outs are for parents, time-ins are for children."

Toilet Training, Early

It is a well-accepted principle among pediatricians (and the announced recommendation of the American Academy of Pediatrics) that toilet training should begin at about the age when the child has muscular control of the sphincter (toward the end of the second year) and of the bladder (a bit later). Nonetheless, over the years there have been those who advocated toilet training infants in the first few months of life. Diaper Free Baby is one of the organizations encouraging such practices.

Although it is not a well-accepted movement, it is gaining widespread publicity both in the US and abroad. The argument is that the infant is aware of its needs to eliminate at an early age and, with the use of diapers, parents are teaching their babies to ignore these signs and not to make the effort to control the muscles in question.

A number of books have advocated the diaper-free approach. Ingrid Bauer, for example, author of *Diaper Free! The Gentle Wisdom of Natural Infant Hygiene*, contends that it is best to begin toilet training before the infant is six months of age. She suggests that the parent grasp the baby by the thighs and hold it seated against their stomach while making suggestive hissing and grunting sounds. With time (and patience!) the parent will get to know the signs the child makes when he or she is ready to eliminate, and be there with the potty at the ready. Presumably, this practice saves parents a great deal of money otherwise spent on diapers. It also has benefits for the environment, with the reduction in the number of soiled disposables.

All of the advocates of early toilet training—and there have been many over the years—suggest the same practices. This is because all such programs aim at *training the parents,* not the baby. The parent has to be constantly observing the baby to recognize the signs of readiness to eliminate. Inasmuch as infants eliminate about ten times a day, this takes a lot of watching and putting children on the potty. Not many parents have the time or the patience (or the energy) to engage in this practice, and that is the reason it has not really caught on—and probably won't. These approaches to toilet training simply ignore the fact that children are biological beings and that you can't hurry development.

The truth is, children do not like to soil or wet themselves any more than adults like to clear up the mess. Children are as eager to train themselves as their parents are to train them. So when children are ready, they will give us an abundance of cues that they want to be diaper free. And if we assist them with patience, good humor, and the understanding that accidents happen, children will be trained easily and without stress.

Toy Play, Sex Differences In

A reporter once asked me about why young boys so enjoy playing with and crashing toy cars while young girls played protectively with dolls. Toy play for children has several different functions. And such play is often different for boys than it is for girls. First of all, play gives children a sense of mastery over a world that is scaled to adult size, powers, and abilities. When playing with toy cars, boys can fantasize that they are driving real cars and that they have the skill of race car drivers. In addition, boys can use car toy play as a means of expressing their creativity and ingenuity. They can create hurdles and open spaces for the cars to fly over at Mach speed.

But toy play also serves a therapeutic function. Sometimes it is hard to be a child, to have adults set all the rules and limits. Adults can also be thoughtless and insensitive when they break promises without apology and fail to use "please" and "thank you," which they demand of children. When boys crash their toy cars into barriers or other cars, they can express their anger and frustration without fear of adult retribution. Toy play can be a safe way for children to deal with their understandable hostility toward adults. Finally, toy play is a way of establishing kinship bonds with other children. Boys who may not know one another may still enjoy playing cars with one another. The activity and their small size in contrast to adults is a uniting force.

For girls, toy play serves similar functions as it does for boys, but in a different way. It is not clear to what extent boy car play and girl doll play is socially scripted or gender based; it is probably a bit of both. Girls, like boys, use their toy play as a way of dealing with their smallness and weakness in a grown-up–sized and –ordered world. Yet, whereas boys feel anger and frustration at being in this position, girls find it a source of safety and protection. Hence their doll play is an expression and mastery of positive rather than negative emotions. Girls too use doll play to nourish their curiosity and imagination, and often create their own narratives for their doll play.

Like car play, doll play can also serve a therapeutic function. When a new baby arrives, for example, doll play may help a girl deal with any feelings of displacement in her parents' affections. Initially, this may even be aggressive, but if handled well—if the girl is allowed to help with the baby—it will turn into a positive, imitative form of play. Finally, doll play, like car play, can serve as an activity that brings girls together. For girls, however, the social interaction often becomes more important than the toy play, whereas for boys just the opposite is likely to be the case. Put differently, in girls it is the social interaction that builds the kinship bond, whereas for boys it is the activity.

Toy play, even when it may seem aggressive and hostile, may still serve important and healthy developmental functions.

Toys, The Best for Young Children

Toys are the tools children use to learn about themselves and about their world. Children learn about themselves through those toys which permit the discovery of their own powers of imagination and fantasy. Children learn about the world with the aid of toys that expand their understanding of the people, plants, animals, and objects which surround them. By far the best toys are those which children themselves create. This is particularly true for young children, who are literally at the mercy of adults. We decide what they should eat, when they should sleep, and what they should wear. Self-created play-things, like toy boats out of anything that can float, give children a much needed sense of control over their world. That is why "watch me" toys, such as wind-up or battery-operated toys like talking bears or jumping kangaroos, are so useless for this age group. If anything, they reinforce the child's sense of being a bystander in world run by others.

It is easy to see how all-consuming self-made toys can be. Recently, our four-year-old granddaughter visited us. In a kitchen drawer she found a pad of paper, a small scissors, and some scotch tape. She spent the afternoon cutting forms out of the paper and sticking them together with the scotch tape. She could not have been happier. We didn't ask her to explain, or describe any of the pieces she had put together. That was not what the play was about. If we allow children access to cardboard boxes, pots and pans, pie tins, strainers, and the like, they will create their own magical world. We cannot enter that world, nor should we try.

I am not saying that we should never purchase toys for young children. Well-made toys, such as the wooden Brio trains, Lego blocks, and the current fad, rubber band craft toys, give children plenty of leeway to use their imagination and to give them an appreciation of their own creativity. Materials like clay and water colors also invite creative play. What I am saying is that in addition to purchasing toys, we should also provide children with the materials and the time to create their own playthings.

When purchasing toys for young children, age-appropriateness is all-important. Computers, for example, have no place in the crib. Infants and young children need toys that will nourish their senses and encourage motor coordination. Colorful rattles, crib gyms, and plush toys all serve these ends. By the age of two, the best single toy for children is a good set of wooden blocks. These support children's evolving understanding of size, weight, balance, and gravity. Large balls that children can roll by pushing can provide a game for parents and children to engage in. For three-, four-, and five-year-olds, skills toys like scooters, wagons, and tricycles can help build muscle coordination and control. Sandboxes, plastic slides, and climbing forms also speak to the abundant energy of this age group. But picture books and music CDs are also supportive of the child's growing language and intellectual abilities.

Last but not least, try to fit the toys to the child. If a child likes to draw, provide materials to draw with. If a child shows a liking for sports, provide toys that support this interest. And don't try to fight city hall. Don't force children to take lessons and participate in sports for which they show little aptitude and even less interest.

Traumatic Events

The events of 9/11 provide a tragic example of how children respond to traumatic events in an era of television and instant communication. The ways in which children reacted to 9/11 varied with their distance from the events, the extent to which they were personally involved, their age, and, to some extent, their personality.

Children who were physically close to the twin towers and heard the noise, smelled the odors, and even saw their collapse were much more seriously affected than children who were not close to the events. Children in other parts of New York and in other states only saw the events on TV and, for the most part, did not suffer any emotional trauma. Children who witnessed or were close to the events, required psychological counseling and suffered anxiety attacks and night terrors. Many of these children still have not completely recovered.

The children who were most affected were those who lost loved ones, particularly parents. Children who may not have witnessed or been close to the events suffered the trauma of a totally unexpected loss of a loved one. Mourning, rather than fear and shock, was the dominant emotion for those children and adolescents who suffered a personal loss. Young children who still don't appreciate the finality of death still suffer from the loss of separation.

What is so hard for older children and adolescents to understand is why it happened, why anyone would want to harm people whom they did not know, had never seen, and had never done them any harm. It is the irrationality of the act, at least from their point of view, which makes their loss so devastating. There are many programs for these children, including camps where they can meet other young people who have experienced similar losses.

The third factor in determining how traumatic events portrayed on television affect children is their age. This is true even for children who were close to the event. Young children, below the age of five or six, have little understanding of the dimensions of a tragedy. They realize something terrible has happened and are terrified that something bad will happen to them. In fact, this is the same reaction of young children in all parts of the country when they see or hear of a catastrophic event. Children of this age need to be reassured that they are safe and that nothing is going to happen to them.

Children of school age have a better understanding of the actual event, but not of its broader implications. They are most concerned about the safety of themselves, their parents, and their siblings. Like their younger siblings, these youngsters need to know that it was a one-time event and that the family is safe. Adolescents have a fuller understanding of the event, the fanaticism that brought it about, and a fuller understanding of what 9/11 portends. For adolescents, a frank discussion of the events gives them the sense that their maturity is recognized and that they can even provide support for their younger siblings.

The last factor is the child himself or herself. Some children are much more affected by traumatic events, particularly when these occur at a distance, than are others. Even so, in the event of hearing and seeing a traumatic event, all young children need reassurance that they are safe, all school-aged children need to hear that their family will not be harmed, and all adolescents need to be given the sense that they can understand what has happened and can afford support to others as well as receive support themselves.

U

Understanding, Too Much

Early in my career I did a lot consulting for nursery schools and child care centers. Once, at a very progressive nursery school, I was seated in a corner observing when a young boy turned from the easel on which he was painting with watercolors and used his brush to splash me with his paint-filled brush. I expected the teacher to intervene and so did not respond on my own. To my surprise the teacher simply smiled and explained, "Isn't it wonderful—he is expressing himself."

I told her, as I wiped myself off, that it seemed to me that there were many other, less socially aggressive, ways for the young man to show his feelings. This incident occurred during an era when Freudian theory was very much in vogue and very much misunderstood. Freud made it very clear that *too much* repression could be harmful but equally emphasized that some amount of repression was a basic requirement of a civil society.

Yet Freud's contention that excessive repression might lead to neuroses was too often taken to mean that *any* restraint on children's expression of feeling would be harmful to their tender psyches. Although this extreme interpretation is no longer widely held, there is still a tendency to over-rationalize children's behavior. Certainly, when a child is under obvious stress, or when we know he or she is in a difficult life situation, this has to be taken into account in dealing with the child's behavior.

But when a child acts out of spite, meanness, or simply a whim, the child has to learn that bad actions have consequences. In the case of the watercolor brush, the teacher should have taken it away, and told the child "brushes are for painting on paper, not for splashing on people." She might also have told him that he would not be allowed to paint anymore that day.

Children are human, and like adults, they sometimes do something or say something, accidentally or out of a moment of bad humor, that is harmful to others. If we fail to take action in such cases, out of some misguided notion of harming the child's ego or self-esteem, we in effect reward bad behavior. Socialization involves repression, and children learn healthy repression when we make sure that they know that bad behavior, as well as good, has consequences.

V

Vaccinating—or Not

British doctor Andrew Wakefield was banned from practicing medicine in his country in 2010. In 1998, Wakefield had published a paper in which he and his co-authors claimed to have found a link between vaccinations and autism. Since then he has been a leader in the parental movement against vaccinations.

After a three-year-long investigation, the London Medical Council found that Wakefield had been dishonest and had violated ethical rules. He was found guilty of more than thirty instances of professional misconduct. In addition, the respected medical journal *Lancet*, which first published his article, has since retracted it at the request of ten of its original thirteen authors.

Ten follow-up research investigations on the relation of the MMR vaccine—which immunizes against measles, mumps, and rubella (German measles)—and autism, involving thousands of children (the Wakefield study used only twelve) have found no connection between the two. A possible culprit in the purported link was thimerosal, a mercury-based preservative used in many vaccines. But the kind of mercury used in thimerosal never accumulates in the body. Also, autism rates have continued to climb, even after the drug companies voluntarily discontinued or reduced thimerosal to only trace amounts in vaccines for children six years and younger.

But the damage was done. Widespread media reports about the study frightened a great many parents. As a result, immunization rates in Britain dropped precipitously, and this caused a surge in measles cases. In April 2006, for the first time in fourteen years, a child died of the disease. A similar drop in immunization rates has occurred in the US.

In 2009, the disease affected 131 people, including many children. This was the largest outbreak in a decade.

Paul Offit, chief of infectious diseases at the Children's Hospital of Philadelphia, argues in the magazine *Parenting* that "We live thirty years longer now than we did a century ago, thanks to purified water and to vaccines. But as soon as compliance wanes the protection we have against the most devastating and sometimes fatal diseases goes with it."

There are still many parents, some quite famous, who continue to believe that the connection between immunization and autism is a fact. They defend Wakefield, as he does himself, by saying that the charges against him reflect a conspiracy by the drug companies to hide the truth. Yet the value of vaccines is beyond doubt, while their connection to autism lacks any factual support. All parents want to do what is best for their children. But I believe that failing to have children vaccinated is putting them at risk for no good reason.

Weaning

For mothers who breast-feed, the transition to other means of nourishment raises several issues. Perhaps the most salient one is when to begin weaning. The American Academy of Pediatrics suggests that weaning should begin once the infant is about six months old. The Academy also suggests that the weaning process should be gradual, alternating between solids and liquids and breast milk until the baby is about one year. By that time the infant is eating more solid foods and may simply lose interest in nursing. The gradual process is helpful for mothers, too, inasmuch as it results in a simultaneous decrease in milk production and lessens the possibility of breast engorgement.

How to go about weaning is another issue. If you work, for example, you may want to put the baby on the bottle and solid food in the morning and breast-feed when you get home in the evening. It is also true that some babies may be ready to be weaned before you are ready to wean them, while others may resist weaning when you are prepared to stop nursing.

The process is made easier if your baby gets used to the bottle ahead of time. You can do this by offering it with breast milk. This not only has the advantage of getting the baby used to the bottle but it also allows others to feed the baby if you are not available. When switching to formula, your pediatrician will suggest what formula would be best for your baby.

Your baby will give you a number of hints when he or she is ready to be weaned.

1. Your infant no longer shows the tongue thrust reflex that has babies instinctively push things out of their mouths, including solid foods.
2. If your baby can hold his or her head up and sit upright in the high chair, he or she is probably ready for solid food.
3. If your baby is interested in solid foods (e.g., grabs for them), this is another sign of readiness for weaning.
4. If your baby loses interest in breast-feeding, as indicated by his or her being easily distracted and taking forever to finish, it is time to wean.

Other practices can help make the weaning transition less stressful for both you and your baby. You might progressively reduce the number of breast-feedings by one a week. Alternatively, you might just want to eliminate the mid-day feeding, which is often the lightest. If this is too abrupt and leads to breast engorgement, you can use the breast pump and feed your baby the milk from the bottle.

Breast-feeding is very bonding for you and your baby. But weaning gradually, using your baby as a guide, can be a positive growth experience for both you and your infant.

Words Parents Don't Like to Hear

Children are little and we adults are big; we have power and they don't. When children acquire language, they also acquire a tool to assert their independence. Children often use words for this purpose without fully appreciating the full meaning and import the words have for parents. The challenge is to deflect these verbal assertions of independence without ire and recrimination. In so doing, we defuse the words without crushing the child's pride in verbally asserting his or her independence. The following are a few of the most common phrases and words children use to assert themselves and few suggestions as to how to respond.

"I Hate You"

Children often use this phrase, or the less potent, "I don't like you," when they are frustrated and angry about some limit or demand that they don't like. Again, the important thing to remember is that children don't hold grudges. They may be angry with a friend and play happily with him or her just a few minutes later. If we appreciate that this is a momentary feeling, not an abiding one, we can respond accordingly. You might say, "That's okay—you have a right to feel that way. I get mad at you sometimes too." Alternatively, you might say, "It hurts my feelings when you say things like that." This also gives the child a way of responding to a peer who says something the child doesn't like.

"You're Not the Boss of Me"

The child's push for independence can also bring out a negative response when you try to help a child do something he or she feels entirely capable of doing for himself or herself. This often happens when we are in a hurry and can't wait for the child to button a coat or tie shoes. At such times a child may say, "I can do it! You're not the boss of me!" This response comes from the child's growing sense of, and need for, autonomy. It is not really a challenge to your authority. Recognizing this, you might say, "I'm sorry I was in a hurry and tried to do it for you so we could get there faster. Next time I will be sure and let you do it yourself." Children really like it when we apologize and give them a reason for our actions, together with a promise not to do it again.

"Mine"

The boundaries between self and world are much more fluid for the child than they are for adults. For young children, clothing and toys are part of themselves and that is why they don't like to share. But some children practice self-expansion by appropriating toys and other things which are not theirs but which they claim are "mine." The need of some young children to claim almost everything as "mine" reflects a sense of insecurity about the self.

It is easy to become annoyed and angry at this behavior, but we need to consider its source. You might say something like, "I am going to take all of your toys and print your name right on them. What color ink would you like me to use?" Putting the child's name on his or her toys and books helps strengthen the child's self-boundaries, and the option to choose the color is empowering. If the child persists, you can then say, "Does it have your name on it?" This then can be a mantra to use whenever the child appropriates something that does not belong to him or her.

"I'm Bored"

Children use this phrase for a lot of reasons. One reason may be that they want attention from parents or siblings. Sometimes children may say this because they failed or were unsuccessful at task or game. For such children, who are usually older—it is probably most common among pre-teens—you might respond, "It seems to me that you are not bored enough. If you were really bored, you would find a game to play, a book to read, or a friend to call." This may not always solve the problem, but you have made it the child's problem without anger or rancor.

Z

Zoos for Children

For my urban sons, a visit to the San Diego Zoo was almost like going on a safari. Many of the animals roam free in what resembles their natural habitat. I had taken my children to other zoos, where the animals were caged, but this was a wholly different experience. Today, as grown men, they still have abiding memories of that visit.

Visiting a zoo can have real benefits for children. It acquaints them with real animals that they had only heard or read about before. To see monkeys actually swinging from rope to rope, or a kangaroo nibbling leaves from a tree, gives them a sense, however small, of a natural world that no longer exists except in limited parts of the world. I believe it helps develop their sense of the importance of preserving animal species and protecting their habitats.

A more recent type of zoo experience is the so-called petting zoo, where children are allowed to pet the animals. This experience acquaints children with real animals they had only learned about, and the physical contact is a bonding experience that supports children's interests in preserving species and habitats. I discovered an even more elaborate arrangement when I joined my son and granddaughter Maya at the Davis Farm outside of Boston. There the animals roamed free, children could feed them and ride the ponies and even milk the goat! There were also play areas and a large wading pool. Maya had a ball.

Nonetheless, petting zoos and farms like the Davis Farm do present some dangers. Animals are dirty and can carry diseases. Some children have contracted illness at such zoos, and a few have died from them. Still, petting zoos—including those at state fairs and now farms—provide a real service and should not be banned.

After decades of zoo-related illness outbreaks, the Center for Disease Control and a collection of state veterinarians have issued these stern warnings and suggestions to those who run these facilities. Parents should take note.

- Provide facilities for children to wash their hands after contact with animals to reduce the risk of animal-related disease transmission.
- Do not allow food, drink, or pacifiers in animal areas.
- Include transition areas between animal areas and non-animal areas.
- Educate visitors about disease risk and prevention procedures.
- Properly care for and manage animals.

Outings to zoos, petting zoos, and animal farms can provide children very rich, beneficial, and valuable learning experiences. But they are not without risks. If you make sure the facility you visit follows the guidelines above, and you do the same with children, it can be a happy, enjoyable outing for the whole family.